DEVELOPING PROGRAMMED INSTRUCTIONAL MATERIALS

A HANDBOOK FOR PROGRAM WRITERS

JAMES E. ESPICH & BILL WILLIAMS

Lear Siegler, Inc./Fearon Publishers

Belmont, California

ISBN-0-8224-2030-9

Library of Congress Catalog Card Number: 67-20924

Printed in the United States of America.

CONTENTS

INTRODUCTION

Programmed instruction (PI) may be defined as "a planned sequence of experiences, leading to proficiency, in terms of stimulus-response relationships." This definition, although not complete, is a very adequate general statement. It also indicates some of the aspects of the programming technique that have expedited the task of education.

By this definition, a program is an educational device that will cause a student (for lack of a better term) to progress through a series of experiences that the programmer believes will lead to the student's proficiency.

The use of the term "experience" in the definition indicates that the student must participate in the learning process. It is not enough that the teacher *tell* the student about his, the teacher's, experiences; they must be the student's own. For this reason, programmed instructional material requires a great deal of effort on the part of the student. Whether the device that stimulates the student's effort is a teacher, a book, a tape-slide presentation, or a computer is immaterial, as long as the device accomplishes its purpose.

"Planned sequence" implies that the person developing the program has determined not only *what* experiences the student should have, but also *in what order* they should occur.

What is the student supposed to be able to do when he has finished the program that he could not do before he started? How well? How quickly? With what help? How do we know when we have finished the education process? When do we stop? All of these questions and others are implied in the phrase "leading to proficiency." If we are to lead a student to proficiency, we must know what proficiency is.

"In terms of stimulus-response relationships" refers to the basic behavioral science concepts on which programmed instruction is based, which are considered whenever a program is written.

The only thing that we would add to this definition—"a planned sequence of experiences, leading to proficiency, in terms of stimulus-response relationships"—would be the phrase "that has been proven to be effective." We cannot imagine it possible to develop a program in a student-sterile atmosphere, nor do we consider a program a program until the students have proven it will work—that it will cause them to have the proper experiences, in the proper order, and that they will be able to exhibit a pre-delineated proficiency when they have finished.

The amount of time that must be devoted to the development of a program will be divided almost equally into preparation, construction techniques, and editing and testing. Writing the frames is a time-consuming and arduous task, but preparing to write them and making them work after they are written are just as time-consuming and arduous.

Part One of this book covers those activities of preparation that lead up to frame writing. The considerations that must be made are many, and a great deal of effort must go into this phase of development. A program is very often designed as one module of a larger instructional system—one small package to be joined to the system at the point where it is deemed necessary for the student to gain the specific knowledge. For this reason, most of the material covered in this section will apply to the over-all instructional systems approach.

The program that is developed using the construction techniques suggested in Part Two is most suitable for the paper-and-pencil medium; however, with only minor variations and a little ingenuity, the programmer can adapt these techniques to other devices.

Part Three, Editing and Testing, outlines the steps that are taken after a program is developed, methods by which the programmer can determine program inadequacies and correct them.

PART ONE

PREPARATION

1

BEHAVIORAL PSYCHOLOGY

No one knows for certain how or why programmed instruction works, but it is generally agreed that basic behavioral psychology is somehow involved. At least the originators of programmed instruction attributed its success to some basic tenets of behavioral psychology. Whether or not someone who is, or intends to be, a writer of programmed instructional material needs to be an expert on behavioral psychology is questionable; however, a basic understanding of the principles on which programming techniques are based will make it easier for the programmer to grasp the concepts of programming and to vary the techniques where required. Included here are only those principles of behavioral psychology that the programmer is required to use in arriving at sound decisions during the development of a program.*

BEHAVIOR AND LEARNING

In general, behavior may be defined as any activity by an organism. More specifically, behavior is any activity by an organism that is deliberate. Such activity does not have to be observable, just deliberate.

A small boy playing baseball is engaged in activity; this is apparent to an observer. The same small boy sitting quietly reliving in his imagination yesterday's baseball game is also engaged in activity. This is not so apparent, since an observer would detect little or no physical movement. Activity can be either physical or mental, but the activity must be deliberate—the organism intended to do what it did.

*For those interested in covering the subject in detail, *see* Edward J. Green, *The Learning Process and Programmed Instruction,* New York: Holt, Rinehart & Winston, Inc., 1962; E. R. Hilgard, *Theories of Learning,* New York: Appleton-Century-Crofts, 1956.

With this definition in mind, let us focus our attention on learning, which is the object of every program. Learning, in the "behaviorist" sense of the word, is merely a change in behavior. When an organism changes its behavior and is able to perform an activity in a different manner, we say that it has learned.

As activity may be mental as well as physical, so also are the limitations upon ability to perform an activity; we do not have knowledge of the processes, or we may not have command of the pertinent facts. If we can attain knowledge of the processes or get the facts, we are then able to perform an activity that we were unable to perform before learning took place. The programmer's job is to remove the mental limitations that prevent students from making desired changes in behavior. He helps them to learn.

The results of the change in behavior called learning are observable, or measurable. All such changes that we encounter in the behavior of students as the result of learning may be categorized as the attainment of one of three types of measurable behavior, or skill: (1) the psychomotor, (2) the cognitive, and (3) the affective.

Psychomotor skills involve muscular actions that require a minimum amount of mental activity on the part of the performer. Included here are such actions as typing, knitting, and keeping an automobile on the road—all of which require muscular dexterity and have to be learned, but none of which, once mastered, demands the complete attention of the performer.

In the cognitive domain, the area of knowledge, are included all of the many mental activities, or mental processes, with which the student becomes involved while learning.*

The third type of mental skill that a student may acquire is within the affective domain. This area is the most difficult in which to cause a desired change of behavior; and, without a doubt, it is the most difficult to measure.

In order to bring about a change of behavior in the affective domain, it is necessary to bring about a change in the student's attitude. In other words, we must change the way a student feels about something. For instance, we might change his attitude so

---

*For a more detailed explanation of the various categories of cognitive mental activities, *see* Benjamin S. Bloom, ed., *Taxonomy of Educational Objectives: Cognitive Domain,* New York: David McKay, Inc., 1956. Bloom identifies six learning categories within the cognitive domain: knowledge, comprehension, application, analysis, synthesis, and evaluation.

that something that had previously seemed morally right to him will seem morally wrong.

Among the many teaching tasks within the affective domain are such items as promoting enthusiasm, self-confidence, responsibility, and trustworthiness, and developing team spirit, curiosity, and the will to learn.

It is easy to see how difficult it is to measure learning within the affective domain. Many times it is almost impossible to determine whether or not we have brought about the desired change in behavior. If, for example, the desired goal is that the student appreciate classical music, how do we measure our results (the amount of appreciation the student has attained)? We can play a recording of a classic for him and ask him if he appreciates it. To pass the course, he will undoubtedly answer "yes," but does he really appreciate such music? When he is in the privacy of his own room, he may very well listen to only the latest popular releases. If he does, we have failed to teach him music appreciation—and we will never know it. If we ask for facts *about* classical music in an attempt to measure our results, we are actually testing within the cognitive domain rather than the affective domain, which was our educational objective.

Most practical situations demonstrate the results of all three types of learning. For example, picture a man approaching an intersection in his car. At the intersection is an octagonal sign with the letters S-T-O-P written across it. The man must use his knowledge skills, the cognitive domain, to interpret this object as a command to stop his car.

The next skill that comes into play is within the affective domain. There are no cars approaching the intersection and no policemen in sight. Only the man's attitude toward safe driving and toward his responsibilities as a citizen will compel him to stop.

If and when he decides to stop, his psychomotor skills are brought into action. His foot comes off the accelerator and hits the brake pedal without conscious thought.

ELICITING DESIRED BEHAVIOR

How can we cause a student to make a desired change in his behavior? And, after he has accomplished it once, how can we be sure that the desired response will continue in the future? According to the behaviorist point of view, on which the majority of programs are based, changes in behavior are accomplished and maintained by a process known as conditioning.

The conditioning process is based on stimulus and response relationships. A stimulus is anything that elicits, or results in, a reaction from an organism; a response is, quite simply, the reaction to the stimulus. The stimulus-response pair is normally diagrammed like this: S ———→ R.

As an example of a stimulus-response pair, consider the following description: a four-inch wooden stick, pointed on one end and with a metal ferrule containing a rubber eraser at the other end. Of course, it's a pencil. The description is the stimulus, and the response that it elicits is "pencil." The problem "two plus two equals what?" acts as a stimulus and elicits the response "four"; and the incomplete statement "George Washington was our first _____" elicits the word "president" as its response.

In any teaching situation, then, the teacher's job is to get the student to make the desired response to a given stimulus—and to increase the probability of his making the same response each time that this stimulus is presented to him. How do we go about this? Here is the best method:

1. Present the stimulus to the student.
2. Help the student to make the desired response to the stimulus by giving him clues, by leading him toward it, or by telling him the response itself.
3. When the student makes the desired response to the stimulus, immediately reinforce that response.

Reinforcement is what increases the possibility that a desired response will occur each time the student is presented with the given stimulus. It may be likened to a reward. Reinforcement is the basic reason we continue doing the things we do; it satisfies one or more of our basic human drives.

Any new stimulus that follows immediately after a response is usually defined as positive reinforcement. Negative reinforcement is the cessation of a stimulus that is annoying (for example, if a rat can terminate an electric shock it is receiving by pressing on a lever, the termination of the shock is negative reinforcement). These two types of reinforcers can be most clearly understood if the positive reinforcement is thought of as an additive process, a stimulus is added to the situation, and negative reinforcement is thought of as a subtractive process, a stimulus is removed.

Punishment after the response is also often thought of as a type of negative reinforcement. This is the meaning applied to the term "negative reinforcement" throughout this chapter: *a noxious stimulus presented to the student after his response has been made.* When the term "positive reinforcement" is used in this chapter, we are referring to *a stimulus, presented to the student after his response, that satisfies one or more of the basic human drives.*

Programmed instruction takes advantage of the basic human drive for success. The programmer guides the student toward making the correct response. He then shows or tells the student that he has given the desired response—that he has been success-ful. Each time he makes the correct response, he is positively reinforced by being told that he is correct; his drive for success is satisfied. Each time his drive for success is satisfied, the proba-bility increases that he will make the correct response to the given stimulus in future situations.

Although limited use is made of negative reinforcement in a programmed instructional package, positive reinforcement is much stronger than the type of negative reinforcement we are considering. Take, for example, the average man's golf game. In a round of golf, the unsuccessful shots usually greatly outnumber the successful ones. The successful shots are positive reinforce-ment to continue the game; the unsuccessful shots are negative reinforcement and cause him to lose interest in the game. It is readily apparent that the positive reinforcement is much more powerful than the negative.

Each time a student makes an incorrect response to a stimulus within a program, we must eliminate that response—extinguish that behavior. The act of eliminating undesirable responses to stimuli is known as extinction. Extinction is accomplished by failing to provide positive reinforcement or by providing negative reinforcement. Each time a response is not reinforced or is nega-tively reinforced, the probability that the student will repeat that response decreases.

Taking the familiar situation of a young father desperately

trying to teach his baby to say "Da-da," let's take a closer look at the value and application of reinforcement. In his efforts, the father crawls around on the floor and thrusts his face in front of the child babbling, "Da-da? Can you say Da-da? Da-da?"

This otherwise normal human being continues with this foolishness until, finally, his perseverance is rewarded. The child, perhaps desperate himself by now, repeats the word. The stimulus, "Da-da," has elicited the desired response. This sends the delighted father into a frenzy of joy. He laughs and hugs and kisses the child, thereby presenting him with positive reinforcement to his response.

The next time the man tries to get the baby to say the words, he finds that it takes less prompting than before. The baby is becoming conditioned to respond with the word "Da-da" each time his father asks him to. (By the same token, the baby is also conditioning the father. The child has learned that all he has to do to receive a flood of attention is to present the magic stimulus, "Da-da," and his father is conditioned to respond with love and affection.)

Now let us look at the same child and the same father some four years later. The child learned at an early age that he could gain the attention of his parent by throwing certain words into his conversation, and he has put this knowledge to good use over the years. Each time he has learned a new word, he has tried it on his father to see his reaction. Then one day he acquires some choice bit of back-alley vocabulary while playing with those "dirty little kids" down the block. As is his custom, he tests his father's reaction to his newly acquired gem. He throws it into the conversation at the supper table casually and sits back to await the results. The stimulus-response pair is the need for a word (stimulus) and the foul word (the response).

The father may act in one of two ways. He may discipline the boy in some manner—apply negative reinforcement—or he may simply pretend that the word was not used. Either action will tend to extinguish the response. However, the negative reinforcement will have little effect, since one of the reasons that the word was thrown into the conversation was to gain attention. Discipline is better than no attention at all, in the mind of the boy. By ignoring the boy's word, the father greatly decreases the probability that he will use the word again. The boy is not conditioned—he does not receive positive reinforcement—and the word is extinguished from his vocabulary.

GENERALIZATION, DISCRIMINATIONS, AND CHAINS

Within the cognitive domain, the area in which developers of programs are most often required to work, we will usually be attempting to teach a student to do one of three things: to make a generalization, to make a discrimination, or to supply the steps within a chain. These three functions are called knowledge skills.

A student makes a generalization when several similar yet different stimuli elicit from him the same response. For example, the student is looking at a parking lot full of many different makes of cars—Fords, Chevrolets, Pontiacs, etc. Each of the autos represents a similar yet different stimulus; however, the student is able to make the same response, "automobile," for each of them. The student can make a generalization.

In making a discrimination, each stimulus elicits an individual response from the student. A person can make a discrimination when he has the ability to respond differently to at least two similar but not identical stimuli. For the student to be able to make such a response, he must have enough knowledge of the given stimulus to make a choice.

We will use the example of the student in the parking lot again. With the ability to discriminate, the student will identify the automobiles as Fords, Chevrolets, Pontiacs, etc., rather than lump them under the general description "automobiles."

In academic problem situations, the student may be required to select the correct solution from among several similar yet different solutions. It may be choosing the correct formula for solving a problem from among many that he has memorized, or it may be selecting the better writing style for a paper he is writing. Each of these situations requires that the student be able to make a discrimination.

In writing programs for industry, the most common knowledge skill that the programmer is called upon to teach is discriminations. Most often, the objectives for a given program will not be so much a question of how to do something, but of how to do something as opposed to how *not* to do it. The selection of a tool

from a bin of tools involves discrimination. Choosing the proper
valve to turn during the course of an operation requires a discrimination, and how far to turn it is also a discrimination.

The third knowledge skill is supplying the steps within a chain.
A chain consists of a series of stimuli and responses wherein the
response to the first stimulus becomes the stimulus for the next
response, which then becomes the stimulus for the next response,
and so on. Each step within the chain suggests, or elicits, the next
step.

A true chaining situation exists when one step cannot be performed, or learned, until the previous step has been mastered.
For example, the process of removing a wheel from a car is a
chain. You cannot remove the wheel until the lug nuts have been
loosened and removed; you cannot remove the lug nuts until you
have removed the hubcap; you cannot remove the hubcap until
you have obtained a tool from the trunk; etc.

Chains are most commonly applied to learning a manual skill.
But many things are learned by chains, often things that are not
actually chains until we make them so. For example, most people
memorize poetry as a chain. The first line suggests the second;
the second line then becomes the stimulus that elicits the third;
etc. You have more than likely learned the alphabet as a chain.
A elicits B, which elicits C, which elicits D, etc. A good way to
check to see if you have learned something as a chain is to try to
go through it backwards. Try the alphabet. The letter G does not
elicit F, the preceding letter; it elicits H, the next step in the
chain. It is the same with any letter you select; you have difficulty
naming the letter that immediately precedes it.

The different programming techniques to most effectively teach
each of the three knowledge skills will be discussed in Part Two,
Construction Techniques.

2

THE FEASIBILITY STUDY

The main purpose of the feasibility study is to determine whether what is to be gained from programming offsets what it will cost to produce a program. Programmed instruction is costly in both the time required to develop a program and in the time needed to validate it. A wrong decision will mean many wasted man-hours and a great deal of needless expense. It is possible to predict rather successfully whether or not it will be worth while to program any given subject; however, this cannot be done without a careful examination of all contingencies.

Before producing the actual program on any subject or a segment of a course of study, there are three basic questions that must be answered: (1) Should the subject be programmed? (2) If the answer to the first question is affirmative, what programming technique shall be used? (3) What medium or combination of media shall be used to present the programmed material to the student?

"GO OR NO GO" DECISION

The first decision to be made in a feasibility study is whether the material to be taught and the teaching situation involved lend themselves economically and educationally to the development of a program. Normally, this decision is based on a number of variable factors, not all of which may exist in every situation.

IS THE SUBJECT MATTER STABLE?

To examine the stability of any subject, approach it from two angles:

1. Is the material something that is subject to frequent changes? Due to the expense of developing a program, it is not feasible to prepare a package on a subject that may be changed

in the near future. For example, many procedural tasks may change from time to time, based on such factors as business expansion, changes in product being manufactured or handled, the whims and fancies of top executives, etc. Subjects such as these should be avoided as much as possible.

2. Will the subject matter remain permanently in the course, or will it be something that is taught today and not taught tomorrow? Many times, material is added to a course for the sole purpose of rounding out the number of hours spent in the classroom. In other words, is the subject to be programmed "filler" material? To answer this question, it may be a good idea to interview instructors who have previously taught the course and get their opinions as to whether the student *needs* to know this material. If the material is not needed by the student to perform the job required of him, it is probable that it will remain in the course only until this fact is discovered. PI is too expensive and time-consuming to permit the extravagance of teaching "nice to know" material.

IS A PROGRAM ALREADY AVAILABLE?

It is usually unnecessary to write a program on a subject for which a program is currently available commercially, and a new program will generally prove more expensive than the purchase of the existing one. There are commercial programs available on almost every subject for which a program may be required. It would be wise to consult a current bibliography of PI material to see what programs are available on the subject under consideration.* Generally speaking, there is an abundance of commercial programs available on such academic subjects as mathematics, English, science principles, foreign languages, etc.

Existing commercial programs, however, must always be evaluated before a decision is made. In order to evaluate *the more expensive* program effectively, write to the publisher and request a copy of the objectives of the program, the validation test, a description of the population on which the validity of the program was tested, and the statistical results of the validation tests. If the program has been properly tested and found validated, these items will be available; normally, they will be furnished free of charge. If, however, the program is a pseudo-program, the pub-

---

*Carl H. Hendershot, *A Bibliography of Programs and Presentation Devices*, Bay City, Mich.: The author.

lisher will not be able to produce these items. A pseudo-program is one that looks and acts like a program, but has never been validated. In other words, the program cannot be relied upon to make the desired changes in the behavior of the student.

CAN YOU PREPARE THE PROGRAM IN THE ALLOTTED TIME?

The preparation of a program is time-consuming. If the boss wants the program "yesterday," forget it! With experience, the program writer is able to estimate accurately the amount of time he will require to meet stated training objectives. The amount of time required varies considerably from programmer to programmer, and it is impossible to give a general standard considering all of the complications that may arise.

IS THERE A TRAINING PROBLEM TO BE SOLVED BY PI?

Many times there exists a procedural problem that should have been solved by a company's systems analysts or time-study men. Because the results of the procedure are not satisfactory, someone gets the idea that the people performing this procedure are not being trained well enough. So, the training department is directed to produce more effective instructions when the problem is not actually in the training, but in the awkwardness of the procedure itself. For example, a certain form used by a company is not being completed properly; so, the problem is referred to the training department. There it is discovered that only about 40 per cent of the blanks on the form are being filled in, whereas instructions call for completion of the entire form. Further investigation, however, turns up the fact that only about that same 40 per cent of the information on the form is ever used by anyone and that the rest of the material is unnecessary. In this case, there *is* no training problem; it is a simple problem of form design.

Other problems often hidden behind the guise of "training problems" include those involving morale, inadequate or inefficient equipment, shortage of personnel, etc.

ARE THE DESIRED OBJECTIVES OF THE TRAINING REALISTIC?

Sometimes material that is purportedly being taught in great detail is actually being taught to a much lower level. From the syllabus of the course, it appears that the students are getting very detailed instructions on the subject; but, in actuality, the instructors are merely grazing the surface of the material. A close look at the examination items for this particular portion of the course reveals that the students are not expected to obtain detailed information. However, when the subject is presented for a feasibility decision prior to programming, it is implied that the subject is being taught to much greater depth. The training goals in such a case are unrealistic.

CAN PI EASE THE INSTRUCTOR'S BURDENS?

While making a feasibility study, the programmer must consider whether or not a program can replace the instructor in subjects or areas that no one wants to teach. One of the easiest ways to gain acceptance for PI—and for the programmer—is to take on one of those subjects that instructors are reluctant to teach. Almost every course has one or two subjects of this type.

CAN STANDARDIZATION BE ACHIEVED?

One of the primary advantages of PI is the standardization of procedures or information achieved by its use. If one man in a company is known to be *the* expert on a certain subject, a good programmer should be able to take this man's expertise and produce a program that permits all personnel to benefit by it. In addition, the program must be usable in even the most distant branches of a company and permit all personnel to receive identical instructions—that is standardization.

WILL THE RESULTS JUSTIFY THE EXPENSE?

Take a close look at the results being obtained by the present teaching method. It may be almost adequate, so the increase in results would not justify the cost of producing a program. In fact, PI may not be able to improve the final product at all.

WILL THE NUMBER OF STUDENTS JUSTIFY THE EXPENSE?

In order for PI to be an economical method of instruction, its cost must be amortized over a long period of time and a large number of trainees. No one can afford to produce a program to train ten people a year. PI becomes economical only after the number of people trained with the program is large enough to spread thin the cost of programming.

WILL THE PROGRAM SAVE HUMAN LIVES?

A man who handles dynamite as a part of his job cannot be correct just 99 per cent of the time. If programmed instruction in procedures or the handling of material can reduce hazards to life, the subject should by all means be programmed. One human life justifies the cost of the program.

CAN PI REDUCE TRAINING TIME?

The programmer must always try to determine whether or not the program will be able to teach more material than the present method of teaching in a shorter period of time. Normally, programs will teach the same objectives more efficiently than conventional instruction; but it is very difficult to compare PI with conventional teaching methods in respect to time. It is often almost impossible even to equate conventional instructional objectives to the objectives of a program. The very nature of the programming process eliminates much unnecessary material, and this results in a savings of time. However, the thoroughness of PI often causes to be taken into consideration factors that were previously ignored, and this results in an increase in time.

CAN THE DESIRED RESULTS BE MEASURED?

In many situations, people who are not well versed in programming techniques have a tendency to develop vague training objectives. These objectives are usually expressed in such terms as "to understand," "to know," "to realize the importance of," "to be familiar with," etc. The term "to understand" will have as many different connotations as there are people who are asked its meaning—and you may personally disagree with all of them. The terms "to realize" and "to be familiar with" are, if possible, even more nebulous. If the objectives of a course are written in terms such as these, it is extremely difficult to design a vehicle to measure results, since the measuring device that *I* devise will not be the same as the one *you* devise.

IS THERE AN EXCEPTION?

Any one factor or combination of factors involved in the "go or no go" decision could lead the programmer to decide not to program. In spite of all his research, however, there is yet another factor that may force the programmer to "go" when he would rather not do so—when the boss says "Program it anyway!"

PROGRAMMING TECHNIQUE AND DISPLAY MEDIA

The second phase of the feasibility study is to decide on the programming technique to be used. This decision is to be made by the programmer only after he has made a thorough behavioral analysis of the task or the information to be taught, for the technique chosen will depend upon the type of mental activity required of the student at each point in the learning process. This subject will be covered in Part Two, Construction Techniques.

The third phase of the feasibility study is the determination of a medium or media to be used. This selection is made after the program has been produced in rough draft form. The medium used to display the programmed material to students is dependent to a great extent upon available production and playback (use) capabilities. It is not recommended that a beginning programmer attempt a program using advanced media (for example, a tape-slide presentation).

All programs begin on paper. From paper the programmer may progress to another medium—if an advantage can be gained from its use. The majority of programs in use today are of the paper-and-pencil type. This is by far the most economical medium for a program, since it requires as equipment no more than a simple mask or shield to cover answers or subsequent material.

Among available production capabilities to be examined are those of slide production, motion picture production, and tape production. Also to be taken into consideration are the capabilities for playback of the people using the program. It would be inadvisable, for instance, to design a tape-slide program to be used at seven hundred different branch offices, since use of the program would require that each branch office purchase and maintain expensive playback equipment. However, if the majority of a company's training takes place in one location, a tape-slide presentation would be feasible, since only a limited amount of equipment would be needed.

3

ANALYSIS OF MATERIAL

After the "go" decision has been made on a programmed instructional package, the programmer gathers material and analyzes it so that he can put it into workable form for the development of the program. The analysis of material can be broken down into three separate and distinct phases: the observation phase, the curriculum phase, and the subject matter expert (SME) interview phase.

The programmer is often called upon to develop a program on a subject with which he is totally unfamiliar, and that is the situation assumed in the directions that follow. Lack of knowledge in a subject can be a help as well as a hindrance. One of the programmer's advantages is that by the time he has developed a program on a subject he has become something of a subject matter expert himself.

OBSERVATION PHASE

In almost any subject matter, the student will be required to perform some type of physical activity. The programming task will generally go more smoothly if the physical actions that must be taught are isolated before programming is begun. These physical activities may be a very inconsequential portion of the task; in some tasks, the only physical activity required of the student is using a pencil. Many times, though, the program must teach a manual skill. When this is the case, the first step in the analysis is to conduct an observation of the task to be taught.*

*For a more detailed discussion of task analysis, *see* L. C. Silvern, *Fundamentals of Teaching Machines and Programmed Learning—Basic Analysis,* Los Angeles: Education and Training Consultants, 1964.

With paper and pencil in hand, the programmer goes to the place where the student will be required to perform the task and observes a person performing it. This person should have the same proficiency that is to be imparted to the student. It would be wrong, for example, to observe an expert performing if the program is to teach only the rudiments of the skill.

As the man performs the task, the programmer makes detailed notes on his every activity. Notes are taken on the tools he uses and his source of raw materials, if any. It may be necessary to have the man perform several times to get detailed notes. Each step of the task, every movement the man performs, must be recorded. When the notes include a complete chain of events from the first step to the last, the programmer is beginning to have the proper material to produce a program.

In addition to watching the man perform, it is necessary to stop him from time to time and have him explain why he performs certain steps. Those places in the procedure where the man was forced to make decisions or adjustments must also be determined and recorded in the notes, along with the man's criteria for the decisions or adjustments he made.

Once the chain of events has been recorded and the programmer knows those places within the chain where decisions must be made and the criteria on which these decisions are based, it is necessary to determine whether the sequence of events as performed is mandatory or optional. For example, the observation notes on the activities of a man changing a flat tire on a car should look something like this:

Man   1. Walks around car looking at tires
           (Says he is looking for tire that is flat on bottom.)
        2. Finds and identifies flat tire (left-rear).
        3. Walks to rear of auto.
        4. Using key, opens trunk lid, exposing tools and spare tire.
        5. Removes tools and spare from trunk.
           (Items removed: jack, jack base, jack handle, spare tire.)
        6. Proceeds to left side of auto; opens door on driver's side; reaches in and pulls emergency brake.
        7. Moves to side of road at front of car; selects large, flat rock and blocks front wheel.
        8. Returns to rear of car.
        9. Picks up jack and base; fits jack to base.

10. Places jack under left side of rear bumper, catching protruding ridge under bumper.
(Precautionary measures: Base must be flat on ground; jack must be perpendicular; front wheels must be blocked.)
11. Places flat end of jack handle in hole in jack.
12. Flips small lever in side of jack to "up" position.
(Man says jack will not operate with lever in "down" position.)
13. Raises car by pumping handle of jack.
(Precautionary measure: This must be done slowly so car won't fall.)
14. When left-rear wheel clears ground, stops pumping.
15. Removes handle from jack.
16. Proceeds to left-rear side of car.
17. Using flat end of jack handle, pries off hubcap, exposing lug nuts.
18. Using other end of jack handle as wrench, removes lug nuts by turning in a clockwise direction.
(Note: On a Chrysler product, such as man is driving, lug nuts on left side of car have what are known as left-hand threads; they are tightened and loosened in opposite manner from usual nuts.)

Etc.

Questioning reveals that it is necessary to perform all of the steps in the sequence indicated with the exception of the blocking of the front wheel, which could have been performed at any point prior to jacking up the car.

The more detailed his notes, the better off the program writer will be. Although it may not be necessary to teach a subject in great detail, it is better to be meticulous when taking notes than to discover later that several steps in a chain are missing. Moreover, the programmer must be sure he knows why each part of the task was performed; his students are going to want to know.

CURRICULUM PHASE

The curriculum phase of the material analysis involves examining the written materials (course documents) that are presently being used. In this phase of his analysis, the programmer tries to determine what is being taught, at what level it is being taught, and how results are being measured. This knowledge—plus a feeling for what is being taught—gives him some idea of the scope and content of his own program. Course documents, moreover, will suggest a sequence of instruction and give some approximation of the length of time required to teach a subject. Another important reason for the curriculum phase of the material analysis is that it enables the programmer to become familiar with the terminology used in the particular subject area. If he is to ask intelligent questions in his interview with the subject matter expert (the next analysis phase), he must be able to speak the SME's language.

The first step in the curriculum phase of the material analysis is to examine a syllabus or course outline and attempt to determine the depth and scope of present instruction. It must be kept in mind, however, that mere presence in the syllabus or course outline is not necessarily justification for programming something.

The programmer next examines the instructor's guides and lesson plans; these documents should give a detailed listing of those items presently being covered. Students' study guides and workbooks will also contain a wealth of information for use in the development of the program.

Another course document that can be used for the purpose of gathering material consists of existing examinations for the course. A look at test questions will often tell the programmer what information the instructor expects his students to obtain.

Finally, the programmer examines all textbooks, manuals, and technical instructions that students are required to use in learning to perform the task. By actually attending class sessions, he often picks up valuable ideas by observing the training aids in use.

In the course documents are usually also found the course requirements. This information is extremely helpful to the programmer. If he is to write an efficient, effective program, he must know, for example, the average age of the students, if it is required that they be high school or college graduates, if some form of special training is a prerequisite, and so on.

SUBJECT MATTER EXPERT INTERVIEW PHASE

Immediately after the observation of the task to be taught or a study of the course documents available on the subject, or both, the programmer's efforts should be concentrated on interviewing someone who is an expert on the subject. Such interviews take on particular importance when the task to be taught is not an observable task, or when the subject is not being taught at present and no course documents are available for study. Then, the development of a program will be successful or unsuccessful depending upon the thoroughness of the SME interview.

The SME interview is held to determine concretely both what is to be taught and the depth to which it must be taught. Since the subject matter expert is generally not familiar with programming methods and the programmer must convert generalities and abstractions into a form from which he can program, the first session of the SME interview should be concerned mainly with gathering the facts. Later, after a list of facts has been compiled, the interview can be used to determine the level the students will be required to attain.

SELECTION OF THE SME

The person to look for as the SME is one who is familiar with all aspects of the job the student will be required to perform. He will also have a thorough knowledge of the subject. Preferably, he will be performing the job himself or supervising people who are working directly with the material to be programmed. The SME should be close enough to the task to be able to distinguish both the trees and the forest.

Management may direct the programmer to someone it considers to be the SME. Occasionally, the programmer finds that this person is not the one who can supply the necessary information. He may be a person who at one time has performed the task in question, but who has long since forgotten important details of the task; or he may be someone who has developed his knowledge of the subject to such a degree that he can no longer put himself on the level of someone who is learning the task.

OBTAINING THE FACTS; THE FIRST SME INTERVIEW

The skill most helpful to the programmer in obtaining the facts from his SME is the ability to recognize and be dissatisfied with a generality. Once he has recognized a generality, he must have the ability to "home in" on it and narrow it down to specifics through questioning. Due to his inherent knowledge, the SME often tends to ignore such items as definitions, purposes behind procedures, criteria used in making discriminations, and the goal toward which he is working. The programmer is required to ask continually the questions *why* and *how*.

As the programmer continues to "home in" on the subject matter, the SME is forced to speak in specific terms. Each concrete fact elicited from the SME is written down. In this manner, the programmer eventually obtains a long listing of facts regarding the subject. At this stage of the game, he does not know which facts are important and which are insignificant, but he does know that they are concrete facts concerning the subject he is trying to program.

The dialogue that follows represents an attempt by a programmer to gather some concrete facts from his SME. Whenever the SME in this example says something that is a concrete fact that should be written down, it is indicated in italics. The programmer's significant comments are also given in italics.

Prog: Hello, Mr. Brown. My name is Jones. I'm from the training department. We're trying to develop a self-instructional package by which someone can learn to evaluate the balance sheet of a business. Mr. Smith directed me to you as an expert in this area.

SME: It can't be done.

Prog: Well, perhaps we can develop a package that will provide the background information on which evaluations are made. Tell me, Mr. Brown, how do you determine the financial condition of a company from a balance sheet?

SME: You compare different things on the sheet.

Prog: How?

SME: By *making a ratio* out of them.

Prog: What items do you compare?

SME: *For example, you compare the current assets to the current liabilities.*

Prog: Why?

SME: This gives you the current ratio.

(*Current assets divided by current liabilities gives you the current ratio.*)

Prog: Why do we want to find the current ratio?

SME: This tells you the debt-paying ability of the company.

(*Current ratio indicates the debt-paying ability of the company.*)

Prog: How does this tell you the debt-paying ability?

SME: Well, if it's below a certain standard, the debt-paying ability isn't good.

Prog: What is the standard?

SME: Two hundred per cent.

Prog: Two hundred per cent? I've never heard a ratio expressed as a percentage. Why do you express it as a percentage?

SME: I don't know. It just is whenever you're talking about balance sheets.

(Ratios on items on a balance sheet are usually expressed in percentages.)

Prog: *In other words, the current assets should be twice the current liabilities in a financially sound company.*

SME: Right.

Prog: *Furthermore, this relationship is usually expressed not as two-to-one, but as 200 per cent.*

SME: Right.

Prog: Let's go back a little further on this subject. We're going to be dealing with people who don't know what a balance sheet is, let alone a current asset. What is an asset?

SME: *An asset is an item that is possessed by a company.*

Prog: I noticed that you said "possessed" and not "owned." Is it possible that a company can possess an asset, yet not own it?

SME: Yes.

Prog: How?

SME: Well, a creditor may still have an interest in the item.

Prog: Is this interest reflected on the balance sheet?

SME: Yes.

Prog: How?

SME: Well you see, the items on the left side of the sheet balance to the items on the right . . . , etc.

At the end of the first SME interview, the programmer should have a list of pertinent, technically correct facts concerning the subject. Note that at this point he does not have the answers to two questions: (1) Which facts are necessary? (2) What should the student be able to do with each fact? (What are the performance objectives?) The answers to these questions will be found through the second SME interview. Another question, that of the best teaching sequence, will be answered when the actual drafting of the program is begun. This will be covered in Part Two of this book, Construction Techniques.

KNOWLEDGE CLASSIFICATIONS

Given any particular fact to be taught, the student's knowledge of that fact will vary according to the depth to which it is taught to him. For example, "The current ratio is obtained by dividing current assets by current liabilities" is a fact. The student may be required to do many things with this information. The programmer does not determine the depth of the student's knowledge. The clue to the depth to which the programmer will be required to teach the student will come from the SME. The SME selects the stimulus that, when presented to the student, will elicit the response desired by the SME. The SME will generally know to what degree a student needs to be familiar with a particular item; however, he will have difficulty communicating his desires to the programmer.

When presented with a particular fact, the SME will usually tell the programmer: "The student needs to know it." Or he may state, "Well, the student doesn't need to know it, but he should be aware of it." At times, he may get very specific and say, "This fact he's *really* got to know." All of which tells the programmer nothing. What the SME means by "know," "aware of," and "*really* got to know," is extremely nebulous. In his mind, he has a very concrete idea of what he is trying to tell the programmer; but such words as "understand," "know," "realize," and "be familiar with" have many different meanings to people who are asked to define them.

To bridge the gap between what the SME says he wants and what he really wants, the programmer must use a language that is familiar to both himself and the SME. He must have a method by which he can ensure that the program will be teaching to the level that the SME desires. To determine concrete levels, the programmer and the SME must agree on the answer to the question "What will the student be expected to do with this particular bit of information or knowledge?"

To help the programmer classify each piece of knowledge according to the degree to which the student is expected to function, the following five levels of learning have been devised: the exposure level, the recognition level, the recall level, the memory level, and the concept level. To these levels must be equated each fact obtained in the first SME interview.

1. *Exposure level.* Often, the SME will want certain information included in a program. However, when asked the key question—What will the student be expected to do with this particular bit of information or knowledge?—the SME will not be able to

find any reason for including it other than "It would be nice if he knew this existed." It is not material that the student needs to know to perform his task, so it belongs to the exposure level. All efforts should be made to persuade the SME that information not actually needed by the student should be omitted from the program. If it is decided that the information is needed by the student, then a higher level of learning is called for and the material no longer belongs at the exposure level. Exposure level material may be likened to enrichment material; it lends a degree of smoothness and direction to a program, but it is not something that is absolutely necessary for the student to retain.

2. *Recognition level.* At this level of learning, the student can recognize a statement or an object when it is presented along with similar yet different statements or objects. Generally, the recognition level requires very broad discriminations.

3. *Recall level.* At this level of learning, the student is able to define a term or state a law or theory, etc., using his own words. At the recall level, the student is not required to respond verbatim with the knowledge he has acquired.

4. *Memory level.* At this level of learning, the student is able to define a term or state a law or theory, etc., using the exact wording he has learned. He must repeat knowledge gained verbatim.

5. *Concept level.* At this, the most complex learning level, the student has the ability to generalize and to make fine discriminations. He has the ability to solve a problem or to supply new examples for a law or theory. Basically, the concept level requires application of knowledge.

The programmer should be able to design a test question that will test the same fact at each of the five levels. By suggesting to the SME test questions for each fact obtained from him, the programmer will be able to determine the level to which each fact should be taught.

Taking the fact obtained in the first interview, "Current ratio equals current assets divided by current liabilities," let's devise a set of questions that will test the student's knowledge of this fact at each of the five levels of learning.

At the exposure level, there will be no test question. The exposure level includes primarily enrichment material, and we do not really care whether a student remembers or retains enrichment material. If the SME decides that there should be a test question, then the material really doesn't belong at the exposure level; we must suggest the several other types of test questions to the SME to determine at which level the material should actually be taught.

The first level for which a test question can be devised is the recognition level. To test whether *at least* the recognition level has been reached, a question something like this is used:

> Which of the following statements best describes the method of computing current ratio?
> a. Current ratio equals current assets minus current liabilities.
> b. Current ratio equals current assets divided by current liabilities.
> c. Current ratio equals total assets divided by total liabilities.
> d. Current ratio equals current liabilities divided by current assets.

The test question for the recall level might be:

> In your own words, describe the process for determining current ratio.

To test the student's attainment of the memory level, the test question might look something like this:

> State exactly the formula used to calculate current ratio.

To this question there can be only one correct answer. It is what the student was required to memorize.

The test question for the concept level would require, of course, much more ability on the part of the student. The test question to determine whether the program was successful in teaching the fact to this level would look something like this:

> From the attached balance sheet, calculate the current ratio for this company.

Note that this question requires that the student be able to *apply* his knowledge.

DETERMINING THE LEVEL—THE SECOND SME INTERVIEW

After the programmer has obtained a list of pertinent facts from the SME, he must return to him and determine the level to which each fact must be taught. To accomplish this, he begins by suggesting to the SME a test question at the concept level on the first fact on his list. Then he asks the SME if a student needs to be able to perform to this level with this fact in order to get the job done. (Is this what he would expect the student to be able to do with this particular bit of knowledge?)

The dialogue that follows is an example of what might result as the programmer questions the SME at this point. The programmer is trying to determine the level to which his program will teach this piece of knowledge: A series circuit has one path for current flow.

Prog: I have on my list an item that states, "A series circuit has one path for current flow." Would you expect the student to be able to solve this problem: "Draw a series circuit, using a lamp, two switches, and a battery"?

SME: No, I don't think he needs to be able to do this. It's a little more than he needs.

Prog: Well, then, how about if we ask him to state the definition of a series circuit?

SME: He wouldn't really have to define a series circuit to handle the job.

Prog: Okay. What if we ask him to describe a series circuit in his own words?

SME: You mean you'd ask him this on a test and he'd be required to do it?

Prog: Yes. If we're going to teach this, we'll have to determine if we've been successful.

SME: Well, if that's the case ... no. I don't think I'd want him to have to do that.

Prog: Well, how would it be if we gave him a series of statements that were close to this one and had him pick out the one that best describes a series circuit?

SME: No. You don't understand. He doesn't really have to know this in order to do the job. It would just be nice if he were exposed to the fact as background information.

At this point in the interview, the programmer would codify this fact on his list with an "E" for exposure level and move on to the next item on his list. He would continue through the list in this manner until he had determined the level to which each fact should be taught or had eliminated that fact.

TEACHING POINTS OUTLINE

The net result of the programmer's labors with the subject matter expert is a list of teaching points—what is known as a teaching points outline (TPO). Each teaching point is a fact with which the student is required to perform in some manner or another. Codification of each teaching point tells the programmer to what degree the student will be required to perform. In addition, the programmer will have reached agreement with the SME on the type of question that will test to the SME's satisfaction the student's attainment of each desired objective.

4

DIAGRAMMING THE MATERIAL

Many successful programmers do not find it necessary to develop a pictorial of a program. However, other programmers, the authors included, find it extremely helpful. A diagram of the material makes the work much easier, prevents the inclusion of superfluous material, and reduces the possibility of omitting fundamental information.

There are two basic methods of diagramming material, by flow charts and by schematics. The decision to use one over another is dependent upon the type of material that is to be taught. Each has advantages and disadvantages. As a general rule, a flow chart is most effectively used to depict a procedure or process involving different physical activities, or "steps," whereas the schematic is used primarily to depict mental activities. Both types of diagram, however, indicate the individual steps through which the student must be led, and which he must learn, whether these steps be observable physical actions or nonobservable mental activities.

FLOW CHARTS

There are two types of flow chart, events-oriented and activities-oriented. Both types normally consist of a series of blocks connected by arrows; the difference lies in the contents of the blocks.

An events-oriented flow chart contains within its blocks the events that occur during a procedure. There will be little or no indication as to the cause of the event. For example, the steps for a portion of the process of changing a flat tire would look like the chart that follows.

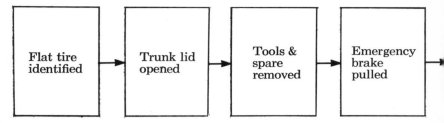

An activities-oriented flow chart, on the other hand, depicts within each block every action that takes place, without identifying the results of that activity. An activities-oriented flow chart depicting the same steps diagrammed above would look like this:

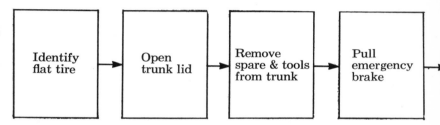

When more detail is needed for evaluation purposes, it may be desirable to depict both the activities and the results of those activities, in which case we have what is called a consolidated flow chart—a combination of activities- and events-oriented diagramming.

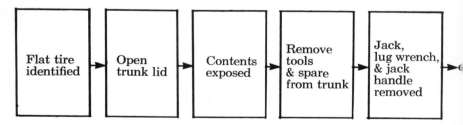

In addition to the blocks that indicate activities or events, each step that requires a decision from which two alternate paths may be taken should be depicted by a decision block. A decision block should contain a question that can be answered "yes" or "no." A positive answer will lead in one direction, and a negative answer will lead off on a different path.

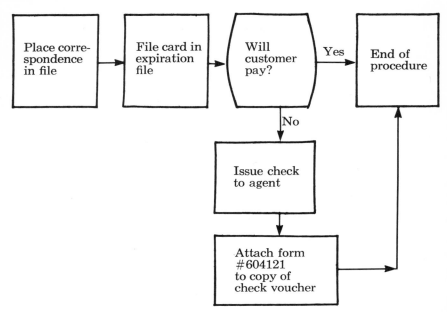

There is no set rule as to which direction one should go with a "yes" answer and which with a "no." Direction is generally determined simply for expediency and maximum utilization of space— and to make the chart *flow*. A good rule of thumb is this: Depict the expected, or the most common, answer as going straight ahead in the normal "flow" of the chart; the less common response will normally take the reader off on a side branch requiring several additional steps before it returns to the main flow of the procedure.

Every event must be included on the chart in natural sequence. There should be no dead ends until the process is completely finished.

Normally, a flow chart is designed so that it flows from left to right. The block in the upper left-hand corner of the diagram will be the first event, or step, in the procedure.

The design of a flow chart depicting the entire procedure makes the development of a program much easier. It becomes a simple process to teach each of the steps and the entire chain of events. For an even clearer idea of what a flow chart should look like, examine this large portion of a consolidated (activities-oriented plus events-oriented) flow chart.

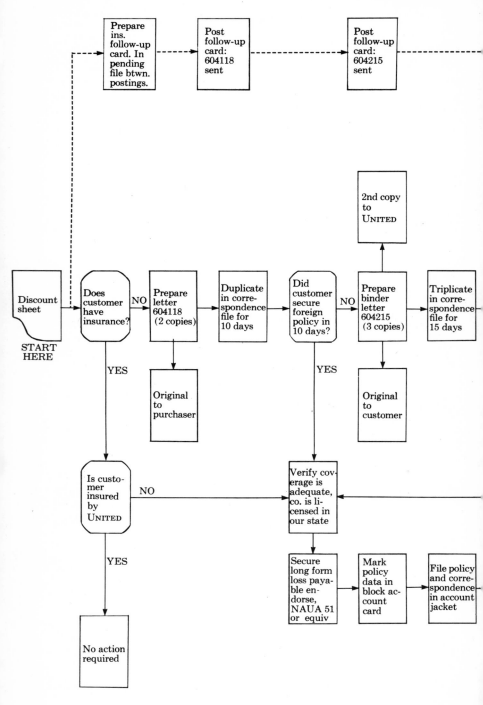

SCHEMATICS

The schematic can be used to illustrate each of the three types of knowledge skills—the generalization, the discrimination, and the chain. Each knowledge skill is illustrated in a different manner. In order to illustrate a generalization, we would picture all of the stimuli for which we desire the student to make a particular response. For example, if there are three objects in the trunk of an auto and we want the student to make the generalization "tools" to any one of them, our schematic will be illustrated as follows:

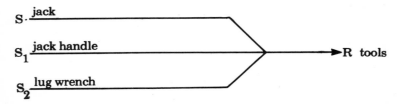

In order to illustrate a discrimination the student is required to make, we must include stimuli we want him to recognize as *not* being the item as well as the item itself. The discrimination of the lug wrench from the remainder of the tools in the trunk of the car would be depicted in this manner:

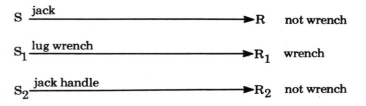

Progressing to the point where the performer is attempting to raise the car with the jack, the process, illustrated as the chain it is, would look like this:

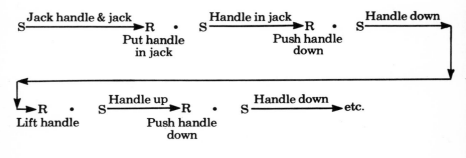

The schematic below depicts a large portion of the mental activity involved in changing a tire.

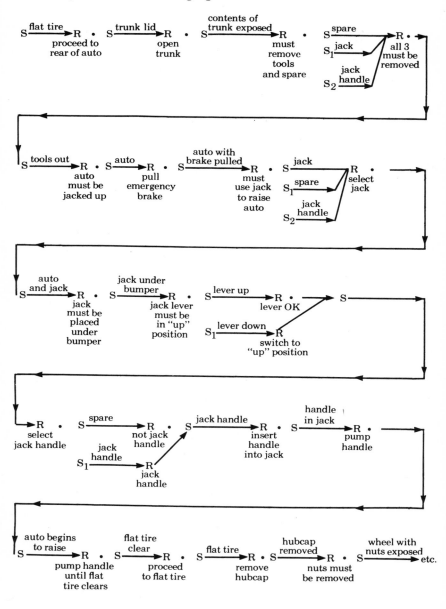

PART TWO

CONSTRUCTION TECHNIQUES

5

THE DISCRIMINATION FRAME SEQUENCE

All programs begin on paper, and the construction techniques discussed in this book are paper-and-pencil program oriented. Adaptations of these procedures can be made to other media according to the programmer's imagination and ingenuity.

TYPES OF RESPONSES

No matter what type of construction technique is used in a program, the student's response will be either overt or covert. An overt response is observable. For example, filling in a blank, selecting a multiple-choice item, working a problem, drawing a diagram, pushing a button, etc., are all overt responses. A covert response is not observable; on the surface, the student does nothing to indicate what response he has made, if, indeed, any at all. A program in which a student is required merely to "think" his responses relies upon purely covert responses.

There is much discussion and controversy as to which is the more effective type of response. There is a great deal of empirical evidence to indicate that overt responses and covert responses produce the same results. A great deal of evidence indicating that one is better or more effective than the other also exists. The matter remains unsettled. The important point to be made concerning the matter of overt versus covert responses is the fact that it is impossible for the student to make an overt response without first making a covert one, except in the case of such simple reflex actions as removing a hand from a hot stove. Before filling in a blank with a word, the student must covertly think of the word to be supplied; if he is to supply the answer to a problem, he must first covertly think of the method by which the problem is to be solved.

Some programming techniques make more effective use than others of the fact that the student must make a covert response before he can make an overt response. One such technique is the Discrimination Frame Sequence, which emphasizes the importance of the covert response and requires very little overt action by the student.

DISCRIMINATION FRAME SEQUENCE

As the name implies, this construction technique is used to teach the student to make discriminations. The programmer is usually asked to teach students to make discriminations more often than either of the other two knowledge skills—which form to complete, the proper tool to use, the performance requirements of a procedure, etc.

In order to make a discrimination, the student must have knowledge of the criterion or criteria on which the discrimination is made. In addition, at least two items must be present before a discrimination can be made: that which *is* the item and that which is *not* the item. The student will covertly weigh the criterion or criteria, examine the items, and make the discrimination. Then he will overtly indicate his choice.

It should be noted that although a discrimination involves the student's knowing background criteria and then making a selection between two items, the opposite will also be true—given the item, the student can list or enumerate the criteria that make the item different from that which is not the item. For this reason, Discrimination Frame Sequences are very efficient in teaching to the concept level, the level at which the student can apply his knowledge and produce new examples.

A student who has been taught to make fine discriminations through the use of Discrimination Frame Sequences will find that he can go beyond the program material and approach the subject matter from any direction. For example, if taught a definition by Discrimination Frame Sequences, he will be able to define it when given the term; if given the definition, he will be able to name the item; if physically possible, he will be able to illustrate it. In other words, he can do any of those things that having a concept of the term will allow.

The two items that must be present in any Discrimination Frame Sequence, that which *is* the item and that which is *not* the item, are called, respectively, the discriminative stimulus (S^D) and the nondiscriminative stimulus (S^Δ). In order to ensure that the student, when asked to make a discrimination between the two items, will make the proper choice, selection of the S^D's is reinforced and selection of the S^Δ's is not reinforced.

To study the actual construction of the Discrimination Frame, assume that this fact has been obtained from the subject matter expert and it is to be taught: Matter is anything that has weight and occupies space. The student is to learn the concept of matter. If the student grasps this concept, he will be able to discriminate between items that are matter and items that are not matter. This is the goal of the training program. As additional overt evidence of learning, it is desired that the student be able to define the term "matter" in his own words.

The first step is to list seven to ten items that are matter—in technical terms, seven to ten S^D's. Seven to ten items that are not matter, S^Δ's, must also be listed. For example:

S^D's	S^Δ's
people	truth
chair	democracy
glass	heat
water	thought
air	beauty
wood	honesty
paper	radio waves
concrete	ugliness

Note that items that will require both broad and fine discriminations have been included in the lists. Using the program, the student will be required to discriminate as to whether these items are matter. It is extremely important that each of the S^Δ's be a logical item with which to confuse the S^D's. In other words, it must not be too easy for the student to make the discrimination. After the lists of S^D's and S^Δ's have been developed, the programmer is ready to construct a Discrimination Frame Sequence.

The first step in the construction is to determine the prompting stimulus (S^P). The S^P is the statement or criterion that will prompt the student and enable him to make the proper discrimination. This could also be referred to as the definition of the S^D, or the information that will enable the student to distinguish

S^D's from S^Δ's. In the present example, the S^P to be used is "anything that has weight and occupies space." By pairing this S^P with S^D's and S^Δ's, and reinforcing selections that fit the S^P (the S^D's), the student can be taught to make the proper discrimination.

The Discrimination Frame Sequence consists basically of three frames. A frame is one step of a program. In each of the three frames, or steps, the student will be required to make a discrimination covertly and indicate his choice overtly. Frame 1, using the example fact, would look like this.

Matter is anything that has weight and occupies space.
IN THE LIST BELOW, PLACE A CHECK MARK
($\sqrt{}$) BEFORE EACH ITEM THAT IS MATTER.

_____ A. Chair		_____ D. Glass
_____ B. Truth		_____ E. Heat
_____ C. Democracy		_____ F. Ugliness

Note that in Frame 1 the student is supplied with the stimulus prompt (anything that has weight and occupies space). He is then asked to make a discrimination for each of six items. Each time, he must compare the item with the S^P and determine whether that item is or is not matter. The *use* of the S^P, not the mere repetition of it, causes the student to learn. Note also in Frame 1 that the discriminations are rather broad. With the help of the S^P, it is relatively easy for the student to make each discrimination correctly. Frame 1 would be followed by confirmation that the student should have checked items A and D.

An important point to remember here is the fact that there should always be more S^Δ's in a frame than S^D's. The minimum ratio is fifty-fifty. There is some indication that the frames are more successful if this relationship is maintained throughout the program.

In Frame 2, the S^P (anything that has weight and occupies space) is removed, and the student is asked to make the discrimination on his own.

PLACE A CHECK MARK (√) BEFORE THOSE
ITEMS THAT ARE MATTER.

_____	A. Radio waves	_____	D. Beauty
_____	B. Air	_____	E. Thought
_____	C. Water	_____	F. Honesty

Frame 2 is followed by confirmation that the student should
have checked items B and C. By the time the student has completed Frame 2, he has applied the concept of matter a total of
twelve times, six times in Frame 1 and six in Frame 2. Note also
that in Frame 2 the discriminations are not as broad as those in
Frame 1. It is a little harder for the student to make a discrimination for air or radio waves, for example, than for chair or truth.

Frame 3 may then ask the student to define matter and supply
examples. He will be able to do it.

DEFINE MATTER; GIVE TWO EXAMPLES.

Again, confirmation of what constitutes a correct response is
needed.

As mentioned previously, this is basically a three-frame
sequence. However, in some instances, it may be necessary to
use several frames like Frame 1, continuing to supply the S^p, and
then employ several frames like Frame 2, with the S^p removed,
before the student has a thorough grasp of the concept.

It is also sometimes helpful to pyramid Discrimination Frames
—in teaching two or more similar items, for example—in which
case, the S^D's for one item become good $S^Δ$'s for another. In
order to teach a series of items using pyramiding Discrimination
Frames, the procedure is as follows: (1) Teach Concept A as

was illustrated, using the basic three-frame sequence. (2) Then use three frames to teach Concept B, having the student mark the answers that fit the S^P for this concept. As he does this, have him also label the items that fit Concept A and which are being used as S^Δ's for Concept B. (3) Finally, teach Concept C, using items that fit Concepts A and B as S^Δ's for Concept C. Require the student to label appropriately all of the items that fit the S^P's of Concepts A and B while identifying items that fit Concept C.

For example, consider the following three concepts:

1. An object is transparent if both light and clear sight can pass through it.
2. An object is translucent if light can pass through it but clear sight cannot.
3. An object is opaque if neither light nor clear sight can pass through it.

In order to pyramid these concepts, the definition of "transparent" must first be taught. Then the definition of "translucent" would be taught, letting the student practice his knowledge of "transparent." Finally, the definition of "opaque" would be taught, letting the student practice the first two definitions. The program that follows will accomplish this.

(Frame 1)

We say that something is TRANSPARENT if both light and clear sight can pass through it. MARK WITH THE LETTERS "Tp" THE ITEMS IN THE LIST BELOW THAT ARE TRANSPARENT.

_____ A. Steel door
_____ B. Tin can
_____ C. Shoestring
_____ D. Windshield of an automobile
_____ E. Man's handkerchief
_____ F. Sunglasses

(Confirmation)

__Tp__ D. Windshield of an automobile
__Tp__ F. Sunglasses

(Frame 2)

CHOOSE THOSE ITEMS IN THE LIST BELOW THAT ARE TRANSPARENT AND MARK THEM WITH THE LETTERS "Tp."

_____ A. Watch crystal
_____ B. Towel
_____ C. Cellophane wrapper on a cigarette package
_____ D. Magazine cover
_____ E. Postcard

(Confirmation)

__Tp__ A. Watch crystal
__Tp__ C. Cellophane wrapper on a cigarette package

(Frame 3)

DEFINE "TRANSPARENT."

(Confirmation)

TRANSPARENT means that both light and clear
sight can pass through the object in question (OR
WORDS TO THIS EFFECT).

(Frame 4)

An object is TRANSLUCENT if only light can pass
through it. IN THE LIST BELOW, MARK THE
ITEMS THAT ARE TRANSLUCENT WITH THE
LETTERS "Tl" AND THE OBJECTS THAT ARE
TRANSPARENT WITH THE LETTERS "Tp."

_____ A. Waxed paper
_____ B. Air
_____ C. Onionskin typing paper
_____ D. Paper cup
_____ E. Matchbook cover

(Confirmation)

_Tl_ A. Waxed paper
_Tp_ B. Air
_Tp_ C. Onionskin typing paper

(Frame 5)

IN THE LIST BELOW, MARK THE TRANSPAR-
ENT ITEMS WITH THE LETTERS "Tp" AND
THE TRANSLUCENT OBJECTS WITH THE
LETTERS "Tl."

_____ A. Frosted light bulb
_____ B. Magnifying glass
_____ C. Mirror
_____ D. Coke bottle
_____ E. One-dollar bill

(Confirmation)

__Tl__ A. Frosted light bulb
__Tp__ B. Magnifying glass
__Tl__ D. Coke bottle

(Frame 6)

DEFINE "TRANSLUCENT."

(Confirmation)

TRANSLUCENT means that light, but not clear sight,
can pass through the object in question (OR WORDS
TO THIS EFFECT).

(Frame 7)

You have noticed, no doubt, that some objects are neither transparent nor translucent. Objects through which *neither* light nor sight can pass are OPAQUE. SELECT THE ITEMS THAT ARE OPAQUE IN THE LIST BELOW AND MARK THEM WITH THE LETTERS "Op." ALSO MARK THE TRANSPARENT AND TRANSLUCENT ITEMS (IF ANY) WITH APPROPRIATE LETTERS.

_____ A. Pencil lead
_____ B. Flashlight lens
_____ C. Clay brick
_____ D. Contact lens
_____ E. Fabric lampshade

(Confirmation)

 Op A. Pencil lead
 Tp B. Flashlight lens
 Op C. Clay brick
 Tp D. Contact lens
 Tl E. Fabric lampshade

(Frame 8)

IN THE LIST BELOW, MARK EACH OF THE OBJECTS APPROPRIATELY, DEPENDING UPON WHETHER THE OBJECT IS TRANSPARENT, TRANSLUCENT, OR OPAQUE.

_____ A. Plate glass window
_____ B. Plastic (clear) raincoat
_____ C. Rubber raincoat
_____ D. Taillight glass on an automobile
_____ E. Wool blanket

(Confirmation)

Tp   A. Plate glass window
Tp   B. Plastic (clear) raincoat
Op   C. Rubber raincoat
Tl   D. Taillight glass on an automobile
Op   E. Wool blanket

(Frame 9)

DEFINE THE TERMS "TRANSPARENT," "TRANSLUCENT," AND "OPAQUE."

(Confirmation)

TRANSPARENT means that both light and clear sight can pass through the object in question (OR WORDS TO THIS EFFECT).

TRANSLUCENT means that light, but not clear sight, can pass through the object in question (OR WORDS TO THIS EFFECT).

OPAQUE means that neither light nor sight can pass through the object in question (OR WORDS TO THIS EFFECT).

Very simple definitions have been used as examples of the Discrimination Frame Sequence, but this technique is not limited to simple concepts. Instead of a short, two- or three-word definition, the S^P could be quite complex; and the S^D's and S^Δ's could require a considerable amount of application by the student in order to make the proper discriminations. There may be, for example, several criteria on which a discrimination is to be made, such as the procedural qualifications for correctly making a book-keeping entry: "Which of the following entries is correctly made?" In order to make this discrimination, the student must consider such items as whether the debits are posted before the credits, whether the amounts are in the appropriate columns, whether the credits should or should not be indented, etc.

Regardless of complexity, if the programmer can come up with a list of S^D's and valid S^Δ's for the concept to be taught, the Discrimination Frame Sequence can be used to teach it.

6

THE CONSTRUCTED RESPONSE FRAME SEQUENCE

By far the most common programming technique in use today is the Constructed Response Frame Sequence. It is the technique upon which programmed instruction cut its teeth, and it appears in some 80 per cent of the programs currently on the market. The Constructed Response Frame Sequence is also the technique most people find easiest to use. Two typical Constructed Response Frames are given below.

(Frame 1) The prefix "kilo" means 1,000. Since this is the case, a kilogram is _____ grams.
(Confirmation)   <u>1,000</u>
(Frame 2) If 1,000 grams equal one kilogram, then 5,600 grams equal 5.6 _____.
(Confirmation)   <u>kilograms</u>

Although it may appear to be no more than a series of short statements containing blanks, there is a great deal more to using the Constructed Response Frame Sequence technique than simply writing short sentences and taking out a word here and there.

As the word "constructed" implies, no choices are presented to the student in a Constructed Response Frame. He does not select one response from many, as in the Discrimination Frame Sequence technique. Instead, the student must *construct* his own response each time. That is, he must supply the answer from his own knowledge.

The response the student constructs can take many forms. He may be asked to write or supply a word or a statement, draw a diagram, or perform any other type of overt action requiring a response from within his own repertory.

At present, the trend is away from Constructed Response Frames. There are several reasons for this. First of all, Constructed Response Frame Sequences have a tendency to be boring to the student. (This statement is made with apologies to those writers who have the ability to "spice up" their writing in such a manner as to leave the student sitting on the edge of his seat in anticipation of his next response.) Normally, Constructed Response Frame programs are broken down into very small steps, which in itself lends a degree of monotony to the program.

Another factor causing the use of Constructed Response Frame Sequences to fall out of favor is the fact that the physical makeup of the Constructed Response Frame limits the scope of material that can be presented. It is almost impossible, for example, to program a physical activity using the Constructed Response Frame Sequence.

A third reason for the decline in popularity of Constructed Response Frames is that the student who learns by means of such a program may sometimes experience difficulty in obtaining transference. In other words, after the student has learned something, he may have difficulty in transferring his knowledge to tasks outside of the program. It is hard for him to supply new examples or apply his new-found knowledge to problem situations that are dissimilar to the stimuli in the program itself. Bear in mind, however, that it is possible to build a Constructed Response

Frame program that will achieve transference. But, if the program is *not* built for transference, it should not be expected to provide it.

Because the majority of programs on the market are of the Constructed Response Frame Sequence type does not mean that this is necessarily the most efficient or effective programming technique. It does, however, lend support to the view that it is one of the easiest methods to employ.

The Constructed Response Frame Sequence is basically a two-part structure, the set frame and at least one practice frame. The number of practice frames used varies according to the amount of application deemed necessary to teach the student to the desired proficiency level. It may be desirable, or even compulsory, to have several practice frames with each set frame.

THE SET FRAME

Whenever the response asked for is found in the data portion of the frame, it is known as a set frame. The student may never have seen the desired response prior to reaching this frame, but he is able to supply this response simply by deducing it from the data within the frame itself. The following is an example of a set frame.

The second file I mentioned is the pending file. This is an alphabetical file, and it is used to hold items on which some type of action is ⎯⎯⎯⎯⎯⎯⎯⎯.

Note that the student can deduce the correct answer and copy it from the information within the frame. He is able to supply the word "pending." Note, too, that this frame is able to stand by itself as a complete unit; it has no dependence upon preceding or succeeding information. It can be taken completely out of context and still be successfully answered by the student. This is characteristic of set frames in general.

THE PRACTICE FRAME

The set frame is followed by a practice frame. The practice frame gives the student a chance to practice what he has learned or discovered in the set frame. It is important that he practice only the information that he was required to *use* in order to successfully answer the set frame. The following is an example of a practice frame that might follow the set frame given above.

Whenever you are waiting for action to be taken on an item, you file that item in the _____ file.

Note that this particular frame calls for the same response as that required in the set frame. However, this practice frame requires that the student have within his repertory the word "pending." The practice frame is not able to stand alone. It is dependent upon previous learning in the program; in short, it is dependent upon a set frame.

It is not necessary that the practice frame immediately follow the set frame. As a matter of fact, the two frames used above are some fifteen frames apart in an actual program. But both frames are necessary, since, together, they form a unit. Of course, in each case, the student is immediately told whether he has supplied—copied or constructed—the correct response. His response is confirmed or corrected at once.

THE TERMINAL FRAME

A sequence of Constructed Response Frames will normally progress from the simple to the complex. The final frame of the sequence is known as the terminal frame. In the terminal frame, the student is given few prompts, or none at all, and is asked to respond on his own. For example, the terminal frame of the sample series used above calls for the student to describe briefly the pending file. This requirement is made of the student only after he has been supplied with the name for that particular file, the construction of the file, its use, etc. He has, at the same time, been taught the construction and use of two other files with which he will be working. The terminal frame would look like this.

NAME THE THREE FILES WITH WHICH YOU WILL BE WORKING AND BRIEFLY DESCRIBE EACH.

Note that in this frame, no hints, clues, or prompts are given. The student is given a minimum of stimulus and the maximum response is being required of him. The first frame in the sequence (the set frame), conversely, contains maximum stimulus and requires minimum response.

THE SUB-TERMINAL FRAME

In the development of a Constructed Response Frame Sequence, the terminal frame should be developed first; then, the sub-terminal frames should be developed. Sub-terminal frames are those that lead up to the terminal frame. They supply the student with the knowledge necessary to enable him to respond correctly in the terminal frame. The first sub-terminal frame will call for a small portion of the terminal response. Succeeding sub-terminal frames should build word upon word, item upon item, until the student has reached the mastry desired—the ability to respond correctly in the terminal frame.

BUILDING THE SEQUENCE

The following is a graphic illustration of an ideal sequence of frames in terms of the relationship between the amount of stimulus and its corresponding response.

Set frame 1
Practice frame 1A
Practice frame 1B
Set frame 2
Practice frame 2A
Terminal frame

AMOUNT OF
AMOUNT
STIMULUS
OF RESPONSE

Note that in the beginning the student is given a considerable amount of stimulus in the program and is asked to make a brief response. Then, the stimulus is gradually reduced and the response increased. Finally, the student reaches the terminal frame, wherein he is given very little stimulus and must supply the maximum response.

The sequence of frames that follows is designed to teach the definition of the word "precession."

(Frame 1 — set frame)

PRECESSION is the reaction of a spinning object to an applied outside force. When an outside force is applied to a spinning object, the reaction of the spinning object to the force is known as _____.

(Confirmation)

precession

(Frame 2 — practice frame)

When a spinning top is struck (applied outside force) by a mallet, the reaction of the top is known as _____.

(Confirmation)

precession

(Frame 3 — set frame)

When an outside force is applied to a spinning object, the reaction is known as precession. For precession to take place, we must have a spinning _____ and an applied outside _____.

(Confirmation)

                                        (spinning) object
(and an applied outside) force

(Frame 4 — practice frame)

Precession is the reaction of a spinning object to an applied outside _____.

(Confirmation)

(an applied outside) force

(Frame 5 — practice frame)

For precession to take place, we must apply an outside force to a(n) _____ object.

(Confirmation)

      (to a) spinning (object)

(Frame 6 — practice frame)

The two elements that are necessary to demonstrate precession are:

    1. A(n) _____ object
    2. A(n) _____ _____ force

(Confirmation)

    1. (A) <u>spinning</u> (object)
    2. (An) <u>applied</u> <u>outside</u> (force)

(Frame 7 — terminal frame)

What is precession?

(Confirmation)

Precession is the reaction of a spinning object to an applied outside force.

CUES AND PROMPTS

The response desired of the student must be indicated within the set frame. It is done through the use of either cues or prompts. The use of cues and prompts, however, is not limited to the set frame. Often, it will also be necessary to use them in practice frames in order to give the student some inkling of the response he is to construct. The Constructed Response Frame Sequence is not a guessing game. The program should lead and control the student's activity.

CUES

A cue is a mechanical aid that enables the student to make the desired response. Some of the most common cues are: underlining the correct answer, placing it in italics, or calling it to the student's attention in some other typographical manner in the data portion of the frame.

An object through which neither light nor clear sight can pass is opaque. A thick piece of wood will pass neither light nor clear sight; therefore, we say that a thick piece of wood is _____.

Another frequently used cue is that of putting the desired response in capital letters in the data portion of the frame.

We say that an object is TRANSLUCENT if light, but not clear sight, can pass through it. A frosted light bulb is _____.

A third cue often used is for the number of blanks to equal the number of letters in the desired response. This technique is used almost as frequently as underlining or Italics.

The capital of England is London. Big Ben is located in the capital of England. Big Ben is located in __ __ __ __ __ __.

Yet another very common cue is to supply the student with the first letter or last letter of the response, or both. This may also take the form of supplying the student with the response's suffix or prefix.

A diode is a tube with two elements, whereas a triode is a tube with three elements. Illustration "A" in your handbook is an illustration of a d   e.

This is by no means an exploration of all the possibilities for the use of cues. Many others exist, and combinations of the cues outlined above are even found in the same frame.

The use of cues is undesirable and should be avoided entirely, if it is possible. Whenever the student encounters a program that makes heavy use of cueing, he automatically begins looking for the cued word and using it for the response instead of reading the material. He is able to disregard completely the remainder of the frame and still supply the desired response.

PROMPTS

A prompt is usually a verbal hint or help, but it may also take the form of an illustration. Generally, it will be a form of transposed iteration—turn the fact around and say the same thing in a different manner. The development of cleverly prompted frames requires a considerable amount of thought and originality. The programmer must be careful not to get into the rut of using transposed iteration in its most basic form in every frame. The frame that follows illustrates the use of transposed iteration as a prompt.

A sales conference is held each Friday. Therefore, on Friday of this week we can expect to have a
_____   _____.

Several hundred frames of this type would surely cause the student to lose interest in a program, but transposed iteration can be used more subtly and still accomplish its purpose. The frame that follows uses transposed iteration, but it is a bit more challenging to the student.

The metric prefix "kilo" means 1,000. A kilometer, therefore, is _____ meters.

In any event, whether or not cues or prompts are used, situations such as this should be avoided.

In a normal deck of playing cards, there are four suits. Therefore, in a pinochle deck, we can also expect to find f __ __ __ suits.

This amounts to only slightly móre than a frame that simply says, "Copy the word 'four.' " A frame must offer the student a bit of a challenge if it is to hold his interest. Nothing is less challenging than an over-prompted or over-cued frame.

DO'S AND DON'T'S

There are a few basic construction rules to follow if a program of the Constructed Response Frame Sequence technique is to be successful. These are not hard and fast axioms the violation of which will result in disaster; rather, they are suggested guidelines the programmer may or may not choose to follow.

1. Always place the blank near the end of the frame. This rule, one of the most important, applies both to set frames and practice frames. When the student reaches the blank, or the point at which he is required to respond, he should be able to respond without reading a great deal of material following the blank. Here is a frame in which this mistake is made.

_____ is the color of my true love's hair.

2. Avoid sequential prompting. This form of prompting occurs when the same word is used as a response several times in a row. After a couple of times, the student responds without even bothering to read the frame. This is especially true if it is the programmer's habit to follow each set frame with four or five sequential practice frames.

3. Include only one thought per frame. Consider the following frame.

Nine planets have been discovered. The names of these planets are: Mercury, Venus, Earth, Mars, Jupiter, Saturn, Uranus, Neptune, and Pluto. Mercury and Venus are both closer to the sun than the planet Earth. The remainder are farther from the sun and thus colder than our planet. The total number of planets that have been discovered to date is _____.

4. Ensure that the desired response is relevant. This frame illustrates an irrelevant response.

We say that an object is transparent when both light and clear sight can pass through it. An example of a transparent item would be an ordinary, clear glass windowpane. The two planets that are between Earth and the sun are _____ and _____.

5. If an illustration is included in a frame, require that the student *use* the illustration in order to make his response. Illustrations should be considered as either prompts or as stimuli that cause the student to think. Do not illustrate merely for the sake of illustrating. An illustration should be an integral part of the frame itself and should always be relevant to the material being taught.

7

THE BRANCHING FRAME
SEQUENCE TECHNIQUE

After the Constructed Response Frame Sequence, the most popular programming technique in use today is the Branching Frame Sequence technique. The primary reason this technique is readily accepted by programmers is because it is quite popular with students. It is generally considered to be more challenging and, therefore, more interesting to the student. Many types of materials can be programmed using this technique, but it lends itself best to learning situations involving a choice of solutions to a problem situation.

In a broad sense, the word "branching" suggests any deviation from the straight line. In linear programs, _all_ of the students are normally required to take _all_ of the frames. A Branching Program, however, allows for greater differences in student abilities. The Branching Frame Sequence technique will present the student with remedial information, if necessary, and will permit him to take steps that are as large as his capabilities allow. A particularly adept student may go through a program in a minimum number of steps, whereas his less able cohort may require twice that number to learn the same amount of material.

There is disagreement among professional programmers as to the actual physical makeup of branching frames. However, there is agreement that the Branching Program offers the student alternate paths from which to choose, and that the path he takes depends upon the response he makes in each frame.

CLASSIC CONSTRUCTION

Branching Frame Sequence techniques are most effectively used to teach problem-solving or analytical abilities. They are normally used in those situations where it is anticipated that the student will most likely make an error. The programmer must second-guess the student and attempt to predict what aspects of the material will lead the student astray. The student will be allowed to make a logical error; then he will be told why his response was wrong and where he became confused. Then, he is presented with the problem-solving situation once more and asked to try again. In this manner, the most logical errors are brought to the attention of the student, and this reduces the probability of his repeating them.

The development of a good Branching Frame Sequence requires a great deal of planning—and no little luck—on the part of the programmer. In a Branching Frame Sequence, the programmer tells the student that he made an error for a particular reason. It is annoying and frustrating to the student if he made the error for reasons *other* than those given by the programmer—the programmer did not allow for all the possible errors.

A Branching Frame Sequence will usually consist of several main steps through which *every* student must progress. In this respect, a Branching Program is linear, since all of the students must go through each of these main steps in the designated sequence.

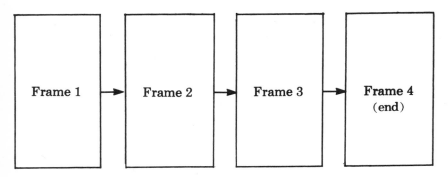

These frames, for want of a better name, we call the home pages. A correct response to each frame will lead the student directly through the home pages of the program. On each home page, the student will be presented with a body of material—a short paragraph or two. Then, based on the information he has read, the student is presented a problem-solving situation with three possible answers. He is asked to choose one of the answers and go to the page indicated beside his choice.

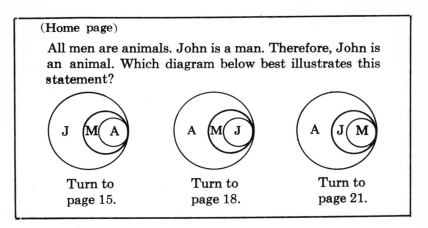

(Home page)

All men are animals. John is a man. Therefore, John is an animal. Which diagram below best illustrates this statement?

Turn to
page 15.

Turn to
page 18.

Turn to
page 21.

If the student has chosen the correct solution to the problem, the page indicated by his choice will be the next home page in the program. Thus, by choosing only correct responses as he works through the program, the student will proceed from home page to home page, and go through the program in the minimum number of steps.

Each home page has two "branches," one for each logical response other than the correct one. The branches, which are also referred to as "wrong-answer pages," will inform the student that he is wrong, give him remedial instructions, and send him back to the same home page he was on to select another answer. A diagram of a branching program with both the home pages and their branches might look like this:

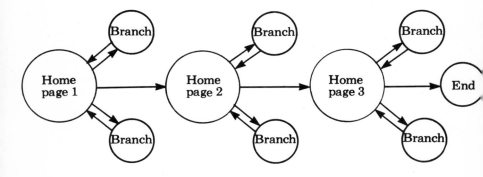

It is possible for a student to go through the program and find it necessary to take each of the home pages and all of the branches. However, it is more probable that a student would take each of the home pages and only one or two branches. The specific pages that a student reads depend upon his comprehension of the material and his ability to apply immediately the information he has learned.

Since it cannot be guaranteed that a particular student will read any page other than the home pages, it is extremely important that no new information be introduced on any of the branches (wrong-answer pages). *All* of the students will read *all* of the home pages, so it is on these pages that material should be presented. The branches are for the purpose of remedial instruction only, and the student may justifiably bypass pertinent information that is included on such pages.

HOME PAGES

There is a definite format for home pages. First of all, on *all* pages after the first home page, home pages as well as branches, there must be a repeat of the response that the student selected on the preceding home page. This is to prevent confusion in the event the student accidentally turns to the wrong page. Upon reading the response, the student knows immediately whether or not that was, in fact, *his* response. If it was not, he knows he has somehow turned to the wrong page. Normally, the response is preceded by such words as: "Your response was...," "You said ...," "You chose answer B, which says ...," or similar phrases.

On a home page, following the reiteration of his response, the student is informed that the response is the correct one. It is the custom in Branching Programs to congratulate or informally praise the student for getting the correct response. This is done by using such phrases as: "You're absolutely correct," "Good job!," "Well done!," etc.

After the confirmation that his response was correct, the student is supplied with another paragraph or two of additional information—the next step in the learning process. (Remember, the home pages are the only places where new information may be introduced.) Then, the student is given a new problem situation based on the new information and is asked to select a response from among three alternatives.

A Branching Program is much more effective when considerable thought has been given to the plausibility of the branches—the wrong answers. The programmer must put himself in the place of the student and ask, "If I were a student, where would this material most likely lead me astray? What would be the most plausible errors I might make?" The answers to these questions will supply the wrong-answer alternatives. A more practical method of developing logical wrong-answer alternatives is to sit down with different students, present the material to them, and take note of the mistakes they make.

The necessity for *plausible* wrong-answer alternatives can not be overemphasized. The technique is ineffective if the student can find his way through the material, home page to home page, by the simple process of eliminating ineffective wrong-answer choices.

BRANCHES

Branches (wrong-answer pages), as stated previously, begin the same as home pages, with a repetition of the response that brought the student to this particular page.

Following the repetition of the response, the student is told that his response is incorrect. This is normally done with several informal expletives, such as: "Oops!," "Sorry, but . . .," "Better luck next time," "Almost," etc. The idea behind such informality is to avoid antagonizing the student. He is told that he is wrong as tactfully as possible, for it will do the program no good to make the student angry by insulting him. After all, if the program is well designed, the answer he chose is a plausible one, one that was foreseen by the programmer.

After the student has been told that his answer is incorrect, the next item on the branch page gives him a hint as to why his answer was wrong and a clue as to the correct answer. It is very important that he is not actually given the correct answer at this point. The purpose behind this section of the page is to start the student thinking along another track and to clear up misconceptions by bringing them out into the open. The programmer is trying to help the student find the error in his reasoning.

The last item on the branch page is a statement that directs the student to return to the previous home page, reread the material, and select another response. If the remedial instruction has been successful, the student will know why his previous response was incorrect; and, after rereading the material on the home page, he will be able to choose the desired response.

Some of the limitations of the Branching Frame Sequence technique are inherent in the system itself. First of all, the question arises as to whether or not the student is ever allowed to construct his own response. Each time, he is offered several responses and is asked to choose one of them. As a result, it is debatable whether or not the student's abilities can progress beyond the recognition level of learning. Secondly, through a process of elimination, all students may eventually get through the material. There is no way of knowing by looking at the program whether the student has comprehended the material; the fact that he has arrived at the last frame in the program does not necessarily mean that he has learned everything the program is intended to teach.

A third disadvantage of the branching technique is its inability to control the student. Behavioral psychologists contend that this method does not shape the behavior of the student the way a program should. The material is not broken down into small stimulus-response pairs that are presented to the student one at a time. Large chunks of material are presented, and it is impossible to employ the traditional conditioning in order to make the proper connection between stimulus and response in the student.

MODIFICATIONS TO CLASSIC CONSTRUCTION

The classic method requires that there be only two branches for each home page. However, in actual practice, there are often more than two plausible wrong answers. In such a situation, of course, the solution is to use as many branches as there are plausible wrong answers.

It is also possible to modify the classic pattern further by branching the student to a wrong-answer page, giving him remedial information, and presenting him with another problem-solving situation to determine whether or not he has grasped the remedial material. Based on his response to this problem situation, he may then be directed on to the next home page, or he may be directed to yet another branch page for additional remedial instruction. The combination of home pages and branches is almost unlimited. The primary thing to remember is that no *new* information is to be introduced in any of the remedial sequences.

A diagram of a modified Branching Program might look like this:

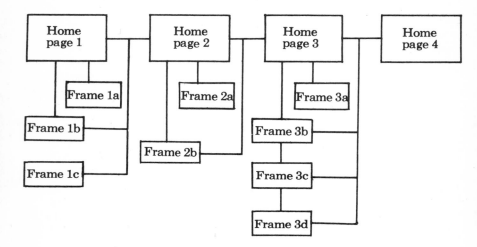

If we were to follow a student's progress through this program, we might find that from Home page 1, his response takes him to Home page 2; or it may take him to Frame 1b, a wrong-answer page, where he is told that his response is incorrect. On that page, he is given remedial instructions and is asked to try another problem. His efforts in Frame 1b may then take him on to Home page 2, or they may take him to Frame 1c for more remedial material before he is moved on. And so it goes through the program. He may wind up at the end of the program having gone through all thirteen possible steps. He will have learned the material as well as a brighter student who completed the program going through only the four home pages; it will simply have taken him more time and more effort.

In the diagrams of the classic Branching Program and the modified Branching Program, each of the frames represents an actual page in a book. The pages in the book are not in an ordinary reading sequence; they are mixed up, or scrambled. For this reason a Branching Program is often referred to as a "scrambled text," or a "scrambled book."

8

RETROGRESSIVE CHAINING

Retrogressive Chaining, one of the lesser-known programming techniques, is used primarily to teach chains. It is a very effective method of shaping behavior and can be applied in many learning situations. Most programmers, however, are reluctant to approach it, either because they do not understand it or because they are afraid of its complexity. The technique itself has been buried deep within the mental gymnastics of mathetics,* in which the development of a program is represented by a series of letters and numbers arranged in a mathematical prescription.

There are various stages of the development of the mathetical model, involving both synthetic and analytical prescriptions, the end result of which is a schematic such as was developed in Chapter 4. Retrogressive Chaining represents the aspect of the mathetic approach that makes it unique among all the other programming techniques.

In developing a Retrogressive Chaining Sequence, the first task is to identify the mastery step of the procedure. The mastery step is the step that completes the task or procedure to be learned. Normally, the mastery step is the final step of the procedure, but this is not always true. In a procedure such as tying a shoe, the mastery step is the very last step, when the bow is pulled tight. But if the chain to be taught is a procedural task involving the replacement of some mechanical part within the intricate core of a machine, the mastery step is that step when the performer removes the faulty part and is ready to replace it with the new one. There may be many steps leading up to the replacement of the part. They could involve the removal of the cover of the piece

---

*See Thomas F. Gilbert, *Mathetics: The Technology of Education*, Chicago: TOR Laboratories, 1962.

of equipment, removal of other parts that inhibit the replacement of the faulty part, and even, perhaps, the removal of certain electrical components. After reaching the part and removing it, it must still be replaced with a new part; then, all of the parts that had to be removed in order to reach the defective part must be put back. Usually, however, the "buttoning up" process is simply a repeat, in reverse order, of the "unbuttoning" process. If the student knows how to perform all of the steps leading up to and including the removal of the part, he will be able to perform them in the reverse order and finish the task. In this case, the mastery step comes in the exact middle of the process to be taught.

It is important to remember that the mastery step, although usually the final step in the chain, may come anywhere in the chain. The other steps involved, those that must be accomplished before one can accomplish the mastery step, are called the sub-mastery steps.

The Retrogressive Chaining technique is, basically, teaching the mastery step first. In teaching a chain using this method, the programmer supplies the student with all of the steps leading up to the mastery step and prompts him to perform the mastery step. Then, the programmer supplies all of the steps up to the step that immediately precedes the mastery step (the last sub-mastery step), prompts this step, and releases the student to practice the mastery step. Next, the programmer provides all of the steps leading up to the step immediately preceding the last sub-mastery and the mastery steps, prompts the student on this sub-mastery step, and releases him to perform the last sub-mastery and mastery steps. This is the basic concept of Retrogressive Chaining—demonstrate, prompt, and release. The programmer continues in this manner, each time allowing the student to perform one additional step until he has worked his way back to the first step in the procedure and can perform the entire task.

The rationale for the Retrogressive Chaining technique is that the closer the student is to the reinforcement when he is being taught, the more effective that reinforcement becomes. The reinforcement, in this case, is the completion of the task. Each time the student performs, *he* completes the task.

The six-frame sequence that follows uses Retrogressive Chaining to teach a mathematical procedure. It is an example of how this technique looks when applied to an academic subject.

THIS IS NOT A TEST.   IT IS A PROGRAM.

It is designed to *teach you something* by making you apply the knowledge you already have plus new information that this program will supply.

Do whatever the program asks. If you come to a blank (_____), put the correct word, number, symbol, or whatever, in the blank.

When a response is required, you will find the correct response on the lower part of the page. Check your answer, then go on to the next bit of information.

Program page 1

---

1. To find the square of a two-digit number ending in 5:

   A. Multiply the first digit by the next higher consecutive number.
   B. Write 25 to the right of the result.

NO RESPONSE REQUIRED.

Program page 2

---

2. To find the square of 35:

   A. Multiply the first digit (3) by the next higher consecutive number (4).   12
   B. Write 25 to the right of the result (12)   12 25
   C. The square of 35 is 1225.

NO RESPONSE REQUIRED.

Program page 3

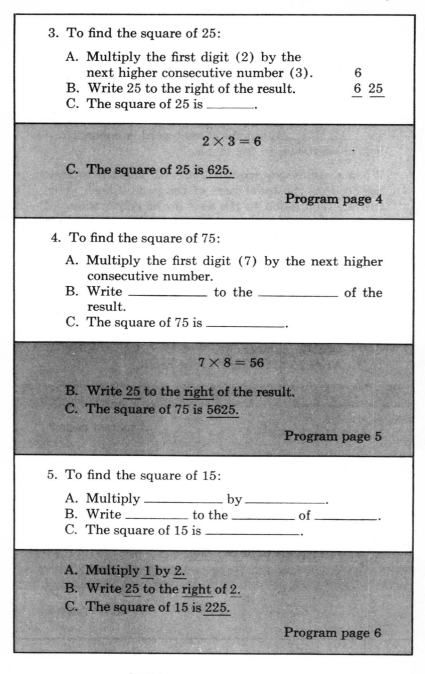

3. To find the square of 25:

  A. Multiply the first digit (2) by the
     next higher consecutive number (3).   6
  B. Write 25 to the right of the result.   6 25
  C. The square of 25 is _____.

$2 \times 3 = 6$

C. The square of 25 is 625.

Program page 4

4. To find the square of 75:

  A. Multiply the first digit (7) by the next higher
     consecutive number.
  B. Write _____ to the _____ of the
     result.
  C. The square of 75 is _____.

$7 \times 8 = 56$

B. Write 25 to the right of the result.
C. The square of 75 is 5625.

Program page 5

5. To find the square of 15:

  A. Multiply _____ by _____.
  B. Write _____ to the _____ of _____.
  C. The square of 15 is _____.

A. Multiply 1 by 2.
B. Write 25 to the right of 2.
C. The square of 15 is 225.

Program page 6

6. What is the square of:

A. 65? _____
B. 95? _____

A. <u>4225</u>
B. <u>9025</u>

THE END

Program page 7

Note that the entire chain is repeated each time in this sample program. Each frame includes the entire process, part of it supplied by the program and part of it supplied by the student. Every frame of the program increases the student's share and decreases the amount supplied by the programmer. For ease of illustration, a very short mathematical procedure was used. Basically, it consists of only three steps. In teaching a longer chain, obviously, the program would become extremely bulky if the programmer were to repeat, or have the student repeat, every step of the entire chain each time.

If the procedure being taught involves a lengthy chain, the programmer must take advantage of the three-step, demonstrate-prompt-release method. In the first frame, demonstrate the entire procedure for the student. In the next frame, demonstrate only the last two sub-mastery steps and prompt the mastery step. In the next frame, demonstrate the next-to-last sub-mastery step, prompt the last sub-mastery step, and release the student to perform the mastery step. In the following frame, demonstrate the third-from-last sub-mastery step, prompt the second-from-last sub-mastery step, and release the student to perform the last sub-mastery step and the mastery step. Graphically illustrated, a sequence involving four sub-mastery steps and a mastery step would look like the diagram that follows.

	Demonstrate	Prompt	Release (Student Performance)
Frame 1	all steps		
Frame 2	sub-mastery step 4 (SS 4)	mastery step (MS)	
Frame 3	SS 3	SS 4	MS
Frame 4	SS 2	SS 3	SS 4, MS
Frame 5	SS 1	SS 2	SS 3, SS 4, MS
Frame 6		SS 1	SS 2, SS 3, SS 4, MS
Frame 7			all steps

Retrogressive Chaining rounds out a complete repertoire of programming techniques. With the addition of a technique to teach chains, the programmer can effectively teach either a generalization, a discrimination, or a chain. In succeeding chapters, some of the less common programming techniques will be presented. Although they are not required for successful programming, they can add spice and variety to a program if used judiciously.

9

BABOON FRAMES

The odd name for this programming technique comes from the response mode that is offered to the student in the frames. The student is asked to make a choice from among four answers: choice A, choice B, "both of the above," and "neither of the above." If arranged in the order of Both, A, B, Or Neither, the first letters of the choices spell out the acronym BABON. From there, it was a simple step to the word BABOON. If arranged in the order of Neither, A, B, or Both, the first letters of the choices spell out NABB. Although sometimes referred to as NABB Frame Sequences, the name BABOON is more popular, probably because of its novelty.

CONSTRUCTING BABOON FRAME SEQUENCES

Basically, the BABOON Frame Sequence consists of three frames similar in purpose to those of the Constructed Response Frame Sequence. The first frame is a set frame; it contains enough information to enable the student to come up with the correct response when asked to respond. This frame is followed by a practice frame; here, the student is requested to demonstrate, with very little prompting, his grasp (or lack of it) of that bit of knowledge presented in the set frame. In the final frame of the three-frame sequence, the terminal frame, the minimum amount of stimulus is presented to the student and a maximum response is called for. This frame allows the student to check his grasp of the material.

BABOON Frame Sequences have application in situations requiring discrimination on the part of the student. However, they can also be used in situations for which a Discrimination Frame Sequence would not normally be used.

BABOON set frames are similar to the first frame of a Discrimination Frame Sequence in that the student is given a stimulus prompt (S^P). He is then asked to apply this S^P to two items and make a determination: whether either of the items fits the description given, whether both items fit the description given, or whether neither item fits the description given. To illustrate the application of the BABOON Frame Sequence technique in a discrimination situation, let us first examine a three-frame sequence that uses Discrimination Frames to teach a definition.

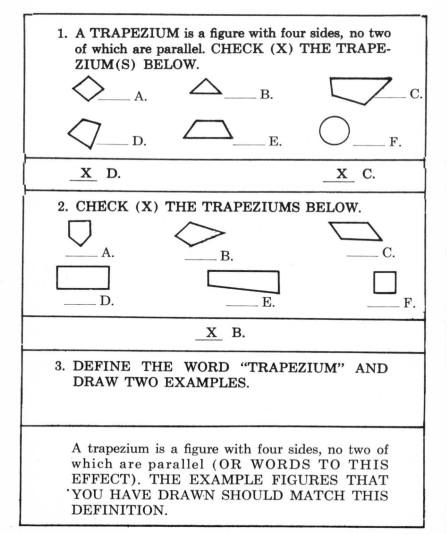

In the foregoing example, it was very easy to derive S^{Δ}'s, those items that do not fit the stimulus prompt. Often, however, the programmer will be developing sequences for which it is not so easy to develop S^{Δ}'s. When confronted with a situation such as this, a BABOON Frame Sequence might be considered. A BABOON Frame Sequence teaching the same material might look like this.

---

1. A TRAPEZIUM is a figure with four sides, no two of which are parallel. PLACE A CHECK MARK (√) BEFORE THE CORRECT STATEMENT BELOW. CHECK ONLY ONE ANSWER.

Figure A   Figure B

_____ A. Figure A is a trapezium.
_____ B. Figure B is a trapezium.
_____ C. Both Figure A and Figure B are trapeziums.
_____ D. Neither Figure A nor Figure B is a trapezium.

__√__ D. Neither Figure A nor Figure B is a trapezium.

---

2. PLACE A CHECK MARK (√) BEFORE THE CORRECT STATEMENT BELOW. CHECK ONLY ONE ANSWER.

Figure A   Figure B

_____ A. Figure A is a trapezium.
_____ B. Figure B is a trapezium.
_____ C. Both Figure A and Figure B are trapeziums.
_____ D. Neither Figure A nor Figure B is a trapezium.

__√__ B. Figure B is a trapezium.

---

3. DEFINE "TRAPEZIUM" AND DRAW TWO FIGURES:

A trapezium is a figure with four sides, no two of which are parallel (OR WORDS TO THIS EFFECT). THE EXAMPLE FIGURES THAT YOU HAVE DRAWN SHOULD MATCH THIS DEFINITION.

In Frame 1 of this BABOON Frame Sequence, the student is presented with the S^P "a figure with four sides, no two of which are parallel." He is then offered two figures and is asked to determine whether either of these figures is a trapezium, both are trapeziums, or neither is a trapezium. He must then look at Figure A, apply the S^P, and make a determination — is it a trapezium? Next, he must use the S^P again in connection with Figure B. He must examine the item, pair it with the S^P, and make the proper discrimination. He then checks, if applicable, the "both" or the "neither" response.

In Frame 1, note that each figure presented forces the student to apply part of the S^P. Figure A causes him to apply the part "with four sides," and Figure B causes him to apply the part "no two of which are parallel."

The practice frame, as in a Discrimination Frame Sequence, removes the S^P and asks the student to apply the definition of a trapezium. The terminal frame tests his grasp of the material — his ability to apply the concept he has learned.

This is a very simple example of the use of a BABOON Frame Sequence, but the technique can be applied to a more complex situation. The response mode will still offer the student four choices — choice A, choice B, both, or neither. Consider the following BABOON Frame Sequence, which is intended to teach the difference between contracts and quasi-contracts.

1. A contract is the result of voluntary and intentional assent to an obligation. A quasi-contract, on the other hand, is imposed by the law in situations wherein one man has profited at the expense of another under circumstances that call for a readjustment of rights. INDICATE (X) WHICH OF

THE FOLLOWING IS/ARE (A) QUASI-CONTRACT(S). CHECK ONLY ONE ANSWER.

_____ A. Defendant, without permission of plaintiff, had taken the thrashing machine owned by the plaintiff and used it for three days. In doing so, he injured the machine so that the plaintiff expended $15.00 in having it repaired. It was found that the reasonable value of the use of the machine was $15.00 per day, or $45.00 for the three days. The court held that the value of the use of the machine could be recovered.

_____ B. Plaintiff sold his business to the defendant and vacated the office in which he had been operating. The defendant took possession of the office and carried on the business. The telephone, for which the plaintiff had agreed with the telephone company to pay for one year, was left in the office. Without permission of the plaintiff, the defendant used the telephone regularly and continuously for a certain period. The plaintiff brought an action to recover from the defendant the value of the use of the telephone during the period in question. Court held that the plaintiff could recover the amount that he had to pay the telephone company for the period in question.

_____ C. Both of the above are quasi-contracts.

_____ D. Neither of the above is a quasi-contract.

  X   C. Both A and B are quasi-contracts.

2. INDICATE (X) WHICH OF THE FOLLOWING IS/ARE (A) QUASI-CONTRACT(S). CHECK ONLY ONE ANSWER.

_____ A. Plaintiff had lived with the defendant under the honest belief that she was his wife. In truth, defendant had a former wife still living. Plaintiff brought action and was entitled to recover an amount for the value of her services as a housekeeper during this period.

_____ B. Smith, the owner of a vessel, agreed to bring a full cargo of coal from New York City to Boston. Jones agreed to pay a certain rate per ton of coal. Smith brought a cargo, but not a complete load, which he delivered to Jones. The court held that Smith would be permitted to recover at the rate agreed upon, subject to a right on the part of Jones to set off any damages he had suffered by not getting a complete load.

_____ C. Both A and B are quasi-contracts.

_____ D. Neither A nor B is a quasi-contract.

___X___ A. Only A is a quasi-contract.

3. What is the difference between a quasi-contract and a true contract?

A quasi-contract is not the result of a voluntary agreement. It is a contract imposed by a court to right a wrong (OR EQUIVALENT ANSWER).

With the foregoing example, it would have been difficult and unwieldly to use five to seven S^A's or S^D's per frame. Hence, it illustrates one appropriate use of the BABOON Frame Sequence technique.

Another situation where BABOON Frames might be used is when the student is being presented with the over-all view of a concept that will be taught in greater detail in succeeding frames. In a situation such as this, the BABOON Frame Sequence technique offers the student two alternatives that may or may not fit the concept. The student is asked to select the true statement, based upon what he has just read. In making this selection, he must understand and apply the concept that was presented to him. Below is an example of a BABOON Frame designed to ensure comprehension of a concept.

A REPUBLIC is a state, without an hereditary head, in which supremacy of the people or their elected representatives is formally acknowledged. CHECK (X) THE STATEMENT BELOW THAT IS TRUE ACCORDING TO THIS DEFINITION. CHECK ONLY ONE ANSWER.

_____ A. The United States of America is a republic.
_____ B. Spain is a republic.
_____ C. Both of the above are true.
_____ D. Neither of the above is true.

   X   A. The United States of America is a republic.

Although this frame may be followed up by a practice frame and a terminal frame, it may also stand by itself, in which case it is simply an introductory frame to determine whether or not the student has read and comprehended a concept.

LIMITATIONS

Compared with the Discrimination Frame Sequence, for example, the student has little opportunity to apply his knowledge in BABOON Frame Sequences. This is due to the limitations imposed by having only four responses from which to choose. After taking several BABOON Frames, the student soon learns that he need only check the first two items in order to choose the correct response. He is allowed only two opportunities to apply the S^P in making a discrimination. Thus, in the ordinary three-frame BABOON Frame Sequence, the student only applies the S^P four times. In a Discrimination Frame Sequence teaching the same concept, the student would have from ten to fifteen opportunities. If, however, the material is broken down into the smallest increments — steps that are small enough to be grasped with only three or four applications — BABOON Frames will teach effectively. The few commercially available programs using the BABOON Frame Sequence technique have the material broken down into very small increments.

10

ADJUNCT PROGRAMMING

Thousands of good textbooks are available on the market today. They are not designed to teach, but to convey information to the student. The effectiveness of these books as teaching tools depends upon the study habits of the students using the texts and the student's ability to differentiate the important material in the book from that which is of lesser importance.

When a student learns using programmed instruction, the programmer has made the determination for him as to what he should or should not assimilate. In a program, the student is guided along a path and given those experiences that will cause him to learn those things. No such guidance is given with a textbook; and, for this reason, the effectiveness of learning from textbook material varies greatly from student to student.

Adjunct Programming can be the link between programmed instruction and a good textbook. It combines some of the progressive features of PI with the comprehensiveness of textbooks. The goal of Adjunct Programming is to enable the student to learn as efficiently as possible from a good textbook. He is to get the benefit of reading the original work while absorbing only those parts of it that are needed to ensure a grasp of the concepts involved.

DEVELOPING ADJUNCT PROGRAMMING FRAMES

When Adjunct Programming is mentioned, the question may arise: Adjunct to what? To give a complete answer to this, it is first necessary to define the word "adjunct." "Adjunct," as defined in our programming concept, means "subordinate to, and in support of." It should be noted that this definition implies that an Adjunct Program is a separate and distinct item to be used in conjunction with something else — in this case, the well-written textbook.

An Adjunct Program may be one of two types: (1) The text itself is kept intact and the program is supplied as a separate unit, or (2) sections of the textbook are extracted verbatim and used in the program as the basic information. The most popular procedure is to leave the textbook intact.

In a program of the second type, where material is extracted from the text, a large block of information is given to the student to read. Then, simply-designed diagnostic questions are given the student to direct his attention to the more salient features of the material. The student will read a paragraph or two and then answer questions on what he has just read. After he has answered the questions, he is not given immediate confirmation. Instead, if he has any doubt as to the correctness of his responses, he is expected to reread the material and confirm his own answers. For example:

(Frame 1)

One of the primary advantages of PI is the standardization achieved by its use. If one man in a company is known to be *the* expert on a certain subject, an able programmer can take this man's thoughts and opinions and produce a program, thus permitting all personnel to benefit by that man's knowledge. In addition, the fact that PI can be used in even the most distant branches of the company permits all personnel to receive identical instructions — that is standardization.

In the author's opinion, what is one advantage of using PI? _____

(Frame 2)

A program is not dependent upon its locale for effectiveness. It will operate as efficiently and effectively in the most outlying branches as it will in the home office. Students will receive the same quality of instruction and the same information, and the results of the training will be uniform.

What is the author's opinion as to the reason for the effectiveness of PI? ._____

In connection with the desirability of using the knowledge of the company expert for training purposes mentioned in Frame 1, what are the limitations imposed by conventional methods of instruction that PI can overcome? _____

The next frame of the program would be the next paragraph of information, followed by one or two more diagnostic questions. This pattern would continue until the textual material had been completely covered.

From time to time throughout the program, short review sequences using conventional programming techniques may be included to ensure comprehension and retention of the material. Reviews of this type also tend to give the material a certain degree of solidarity and wholeness.

The other type of Adjunct Programming, using the text intact and providing the student with the program as a separate unit to be used in conjunction with the text, may take either of two forms. First, it may be similar to the type detailed above, in that the student is asked to leave the program and read a paragraph or two in the book. After reading, he must return to the program to answer one or two diagnostic questions covering the salient features of those paragraphs. He is then redirected to the book to read another section, after which he returns to the program to answer more questions. This method is not unique in itself, in as much as it closely resembles the commonly-used summary questions at the end of textbook chapters. Like summary questions, too, it can increase the effectiveness of a text.

The second form that a program of this type might take is one more typical of programmed instruction. The student is directed to leave the program and read an entire chapter or section of the text. Then he returns to the program and is given a succinct programmed sequence, with normal response confirmation, that reteaches, in large steps, the most important features of the passage. This program is developed against distinct terminal achievement objectives, and it is designed to ensure that the student learns what he needs to know from the chapter.

It is also possible to use a form of the Adjunct Programming technique in a program that otherwise uses conventional programming methods. By utilizing special branching techniques, it is possible to branch the student from the program to a chapter in a conventional text to enable him to answer one of the questions or problem situations presented within the program. The student is asked within the program to respond to a question, the answer to which he has not been previously provided. He is then instructed to go to a conventional textbook and read a passage, a chapter, or perhaps the entire book. Then he returns to the program, makes the requested response, and proceeds along his learning path. In addition to being branched to read material in a text, the student may also be branched to conduct an experiment, make a field trip, make a study, or any number of other activities. In a situation such as this, the textbook, experiment, etc., are adjuncts to the program—a reversal of the usual procedure.

An Adjunct Program can be written to supplement almost any conventional textbook without changing the textbook author's words. Books, of course, are protected by copyright laws, and any unauthorized use of them is in violation of these laws. However, since an Adjunct Program normally implies that a textbook must be purchased as the basic information for the program, an author should welcome the use of his book and grant permission for such an endeavor.

11

ADJUSTIVE DEVICES

Within most groups for which programs are to be written, the students will have varied backgrounds and abilities. The programmer's task is to design a package that will fit the group as a whole. At times this may be a very difficult thing to do, especially if the program is intended for the general public. The task can be just as difficult for the programmer in industry who must design programs that will train someone for a position for which there are few prerequisite skills, such as a cashier, a clerk, an unskilled production line job, etc.

The new program may be for use as an instructional device for persons who are entirely new to the material to be taught. Just as often, however, the program may be used by persons who are experienced in a particular skill, but who feel they need to brush up. Programmed instruction may be boring to a student who already knows the material being taught. This holds true for every functional program on the market, since programs are designed primarily to teach, not to entertain. Too often, a program is judged by someone who is already familiar with the subject matter it covers. In such a situation, the natural evaluation of the program is that it takes ridiculously small steps, is monotonous, and insults the student's intelligence. Of course it does and is—to someone who knew the material before he read the first frame. But to someone who is entirely unfamiliar with the subject matter, the size of the step may be exactly what he needs. As a corollary to this reaction, once a student learns one of the concepts in a program, any further effort to teach him this same thing causes him to become impatient and to find the program distasteful.

A good program, then, will allow the student to progress as quickly and with as large a step as he can safely and effectively handle. This is the purpose of the adjustive device—to compensate for the differences in backgrounds, learning abilities, and capacities of the various students who make up a group, and, thereby, allow each student to adjust his progress according to his own needs.

GROUP DIFFERENCES

One of the first factors to consider when preparing a program is the age spread of the group. A wide latitude in ages will normally produce a proportionately wide difference in learning abilities. This is a result of several factors. A person who has been out of school for many years is not as accustomed to studying and learning as someone fresh out of high school or college. Certain skills upon which the program may depend, such as mathematical ability, composition, finger dexterity, etc., may not be as efficient in older persons; they may have forgotten how to divide fractions or calculate a ratio, find the square root of a three-digit number, etc. On the other hand, this more mature person will probably be more studious and work harder. It is the programmer's responsibility to use an adjustive device to refresh those older students who need refreshing—but only those who *need* refreshing.

Another factor that may require adjustive devices in the program is the educational-level spread of the group. Differences here will most likely be reflected in the size of the concept that the student is capable of grasping. Normally, as a student progresses in school, his verbal abilities become greater and he can more easily comprehend complex ideas and concepts. Conversely, simpler ideas tend to insult or bore him.

Mathematical ability might also be considered in connection with the educational-level spread of the group. In science, in particular, the depth to which a program can take a person in the exploration of an idea or concept is most likely limited by the level of mathematics that the student can handle. The mathematical skills within a group will vary according to its members' educational levels, and a program will be better if it can compensate for the differences.

Another consideration to be made with respect to the educational-level spread within a group is the vocabulary that is already a part of each student's repertory. Does he need to be taught the meanings of certain words, or can the programmer assume that he knows the words and go on to teach something else? Adjustments for vocabulary differences may be desirable.

Within most groups, there will be a mixture of the sexes. Certain concepts seem to be more easily grasped by men than by women, and vice versa. Allowances may have to be made for any variance. Examples and vocabulary must also be taken into consideration when dealing with a mixed group. In any case, the program should detect any differences existing in a group consisting of both sexes and compensate for them.

The type of work previously engaged in by the students may also be a relevant factor. If it can be assured that all of them have performed certain tasks or held certain jobs, the programmer may assume that certain knowledge items are a part of his students' abilities. However, the program should also allow for the inadequacies of those people who do not have the prerequisite skills.

Generally, the population spread for which a program is to be written will be wide. There will be extremes in all of the categories that have been mentioned. For this reason, adjustive devices are required to help the program do its job most effectively.

TYPES OF ADJUSTIVE DEVICES

BRANCHING PROGRAMS

Any kind of Branching Program is an adjustive device, for the very purpose of the branch in a Branching Frame Sequence is to give remedial instruction to the slower student. As a brief review, consider the following diagram:

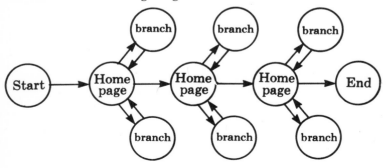

The quicker students progress through the material in leaps and bounds—taking the maximum-sized steps, requiring only a minimum of instruction, and ignoring completely the remedial frames. The slower learners get additional instruction through the various branches of the program. They may require three times the number of frames to learn the material as well as their brighter peers. The program has the ability to give them this much-needed additional instruction.

GATE FRAMES

A gate frame is a frame that directs the student to a different portion of a linear program, depending upon his ability to grasp certain information. The gate frame may allow the student to skip ahead several frames; it may also send him back to review certain material.

Frames of this type should not be confused with branching frames. The remedial frames in a Branching Frame Sequence redirect the student to the home page after he has been given his remedial instruction. A gate frame merely allows the student to skip ahead and bypass material that he does not need to study, or it sends him back for a review.

There are two types of gate frames, wash-ahead frames and wash-back frames. The wash-ahead frame sends the student ahead, allowing him to skip a few frames; and the wash-back frame sends him back to review material previously covered. Here is an example of a wash-ahead gate frame.

---

26. Lesson objectives should be written in behavioral terms. Which of the following is a good lesson objective?

A. The student will be familiar with Ohm's Law. (Turn to Frame 27.)
B. Given two of the three parameters of a circuit, the student will be able to use Ohm's Law to solve for the unknown. (Turn to Frame 33.)

The diagram of part of a program below illustrates the use of gate frames.

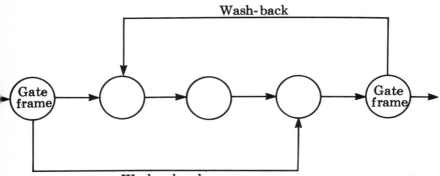

REMEDIAL LOOPS

A remedial loop is a form of branching, but it is slightly different from the normal Branching Frame Sequence technique. In its usual form, a Branching Frame Sequence takes the student off the main track of the program, gives him one frame of remedial instruction, and sends him back to the frame from which he came. The remedial loop directs the student off the main track of the program and gives him a *series* of frames that supply him with knowledge he lacks at that point in the program. A diagram of a remedial loop adjustive device might look like this:

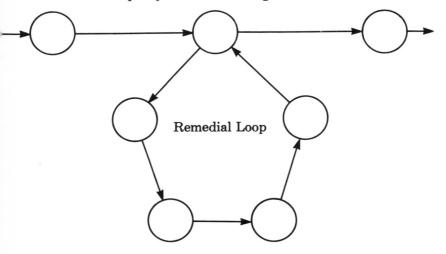

A remedial loop within a program may consist of five or six frames; it supplies the student with additional instruction or explanation. However, a remedial loop may be an entire program, if required. It is important to note that a remedial loop will not include any information that *all* of the students need. Just as with the remedial branch in a Branching Program, there is no way of knowing whether or not the students will take the frames in the remedial loop.

The remedial loop itself may be physically located anywhere in a program. Usually, however, this sequence of frames will be included at the end of a section or at the end of the entire program; and the student will, of course, be referred to the loop with a frame similar to a gate frame. The last frame of the loop will direct him back to the frame from which he came.

SECONDARY TRACKS

In this type of adjustive device, the student is offered, in each frame, three individual tracks—Track A, Track B, and Track C. The student reads the information in Track A and responds, if he feels that he can. He is directed in the instructions that if, after reading Track A, he still does not thoroughly understand the material, he is to drop down and read Track B, which is a repeat of Track A in simpler terms—that is, in smaller steps. If the student makes this choice and drops down to Track B, he may make a response, then go on to the next frame. However, if he still does not think his grasp of the material is what it should be, he may drop down to Track C and receive even more detailed information. In this manner, the student proceeds, taking only Track A of each frame, or taking any of the many possible track combinations in working his way through the program. The example that follows is a page from a program using secondary tracks.

TRACK A	39. If velocity is expressed in feet per second and acceleration is expressed in velocity per second, the expression that will be used for acceleration is:_____

TRACK B	If velocity is expressed in feet per second and acceleration is expressed in velocity per second, the expression that will be used for acceleration is: _____ A. Seconds per feet. _____ B. Feet per second. _____ C. Feet per second per second. _____ D. Foot-seconds per second.

TRACK C	Velocity is expressed in feet per second—that is, the number of feet that a moving object moves in one second. Acceleration is velocity per second. If we were trying to find a way to express acceleration, we could substitute in our definition of velocity per second the equivalent of velocity, or "feet per second." The resulting expression would then be feet $\underset{\text{velocity}}{\underline{\text{per second}}}$/per second. NO RESPONSE REQUIRED.

In this particular frame, Track C does not call for a response from the student. If it did, the response would normally be simpler than the one called for in Track B.

The following is a diagram of the secondary track adjustive device:

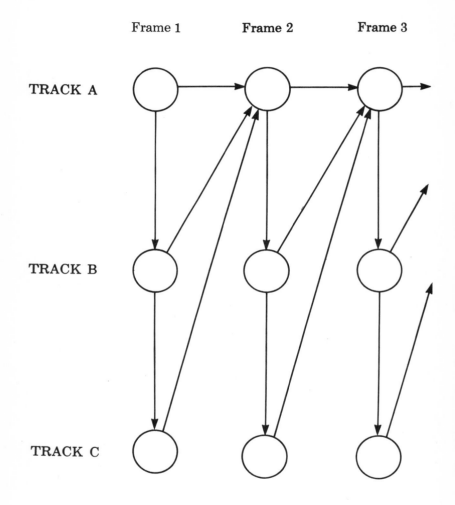

SCHEMATIC DIAGRAMS

When using adjustive devices, it is helpful to lay out the program in schematic form prior to numbering the pages or frames. A diagram of this type will ensure that the student is not led into blind corners at any point or allowed to skip essential information. The diagram below is a hypothetical example of a program that uses all of the adjustive devices discussed in this chapter.

BRANCHING   **GATE FRAMES**

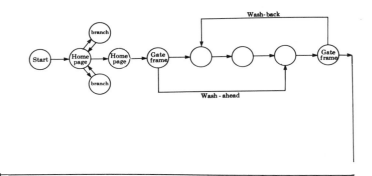

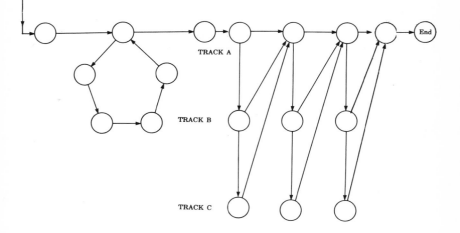

REMEDIAL LOOP   **SECONDARY TRACKS**

DO'S AND DON'T'S

The adjustive devices presented in this chapter do not cover the entire spectrum of things that can be done in a program to compensate for student differences; they apply primarily to programs presented on paper. If other media are used, the possibilities for variation are much greater.

As a general rule, two things must be kept constantly in mind when designing adjustive devices. First, the student must be able to find his way through the maze with a certain degree of facility. Do not load him down with a page and a half of instructions regarding what to do in various and sundry situations. Keep the directions simple and supply him with instructions within the frames themselves as to where he is to go from where he is.

The second thing to remember, and this cannot be repeated too often: Do not include *only* in a remedial instructive device any information that is required by *all* of the students. If an alternate path through the material is available to the student, a path that does not contain the essential information, it would not be fair to hold the student responsible for this information.

Adjustive devices can make a program work more efficiently. Proper use of these devices can also make a program more interesting and challenging to the faster student, while not leaving behind, hopelessly confused, the slower student.

PART THREE

EDITING AND TESTING

12

THE PROGRAM EDIT

A thorough program edit may uncover many program inadequacies prior to testing. The edit can result in a smoothness that may make the difference between the success or failure of the program.

There are three types of editing involved with a program: editing for composition, editing for programming technique, and editing for technical accuracy.

COMPOSITION EDIT

Editing a program for composition is the same as editing any other written material for composition. The program is checked for grammar, language, spelling, the ability to communicate, aptness of examples, and punctuation. Also examined are such mechanical aspects of the material as the length of blanks, uniformity of numbering systems, placement of illustrations, and adherence to some basic construction rules.

The entire program will present a more favorable appearance to the student if it is compositionally correct. Errors will probably influence some students to think poorly of the program and to question the ability of the programmer. The student's reaction might be, "How's this guy going to teach me anything? He can't even spell or punctuate a sentence!"

A second factor that requires emphasis is the importance of maintaining a consistency throughout the program from the standpoint of what the student is expected to do. As an illustration of this, a program may contain Discrimination Frames, wherein the student is to check *all applicable* responses, and BABOON Frames, in which he is to check *only one* of the responses presented. It will be easier for the student if he is able to differentiate at first glance the Discrimination Frames from the BABOON Frames.

If necessary, the student should be instructed within each frame as to what his action should be. If one Discrimination Frame tells him to put an "X" in the space to the left of each correct response, then *all* discrimination frames in the program should ask him to do this. Needless to say, it is confusing to the student to be asked to make a check mark in one frame, to make an "X" in the next, and to circle the correct answer in a third.

Some basic construction rules appear in the Appendix. They are offered solely as guidelines and not as required procedure. The important thing is to use *somebody's* rules and follow them religiously throughout each program. A programmer may develop his own style guide to suit his own particular types of programs, but he must be consistent throughout each of the programs that he develops.

Learning through programmed instruction is a very arduous task for the student. Leading him through a maze of difficult frame formats, response modes, and mechanics will only compound his problems. Programs are supposed to make the student think, but they are supposed to make him think about the material being taught and not about such things as "Where do I go from here?"

PROGRAMMING TECHNIQUE
EDIT—THE PROGRAM

Several aspects of technique editing apply to the program as a whole. The continuity of the program is one of them. The program must flow from item to item. Is there an interrelationship between the parts of the program? Is the program composed of individual, unrelated sequences? If so, the continuity could stand improvement.

The programmer should also ask himself some questions about the development of ideas within his program. Are they logically and methodically developed, with an adequate amount of supporting material? Have examples been used aptly to develop ideas? Are the examples things with which this student population is familiar? Can the students follow the line of reasoning throughout the program as the material is developed? Does the program work steadily toward a conclusion? These items should be considered very thoroughly, for they can make the difference between a program that appeals to the student and one that frustrates him.

Another consideration to be made during a general program technique edit is the size of the steps within the program. Too large a step size will lose the student, and too small a step size may drive him to distraction. The optimum step size for a particular student population can only be guessed at, but the programmer must try to tailor his steps to fit his group.

Two different types of step sizes must be considered, the *inter*-frame and the *intra*-frame. Inter-frame step size is the size of the step from one frame to the next: How big a jump is being taken from teaching point to teaching point? The intra-frame step size is the size of the concept presented within a single frame: How much is the student expected to grasp in each frame? How difficult is it for him to apply the knowledge presented as he responds to the frame? This will be discussed later in greater detail.

Another consideration during the technique edit of the program in general is, of course, whether or not the rules of construction technique were followed throughout the program. In the course of writing and rewriting, it is possible that a frame or two may have been left out inadvertently. Items to check for include: practice frames with no set frames, practice frames that have been placed ahead of their respective set frames, terminal frames out of sequence, a frame sequence incomplete, etc.

The final aspect of the technique edit of the program is the quality and aptness of the illustrations used. The placement of illustrations in relation to printed matter may also be a factor. Guidelines for the use of illustrations are found in the Appendix.

PROGRAMMING TECHNIQUE
EDIT—THE FRAMES

The purpose of the individual frame edit is to catch obvious faults before they affect the performance of the program. A frame evaluation that considers several frames individually, with no regard to the material that preceded each frame or is to follow it, may not be valid. In considering a frame individually, inadequacies are suspected that exist only when that frame is taken out of context. Earlier frames may have precluded the inadequacies. However, much benefit can be gained from examining each frame individually and deliberately looking for inadequacies.

Illustrations should be used whenever applicable in a program, but the frame in which an illustration is used must be so designed that the student is forced to make use of the illustration in one manner or another before forming his response. One picture may be worth a thousand words—but *only* if the programmer can be sure the student looks at it. If the student can answer the frame without consulting a particular illustration, the programmer cannot be sure the student is going to look at it. If he has included a concept or idea in that illustration that is important to the outcome of the program, and he should have, he must make sure that the student will look at it.

So, the programmer must ask himself about the illustration in any frame: (1) Is the illustration meaningful? (2) Is the student required to use the illustration to make his response? If the answer to either of these questions is negative, the need for the particular illustration is dubious.

Along this same line, it is wise to check the quality of the artwork. The programmer should show an illustration to several people and ask them what they think it depicts. If it is intended to illustrate motion, he should get several opinions as to which direction and what type of motion it depicts. An illustration that conveys something other than what the programmer intends can do more *harm* than a thousand words.

The next step in a frame edit is to take a close look at the response required of the student. Is the response he makes relevant? It is a good rule never to have the student respond with anything he is not supposed to learn. For maximum program efficiency and effectiveness, each response the student makes should be a part of the terminal behavior toward which he is being led.

In addition to the relevancy of the response, careful consideration should be made of the response mode that is used. Is the student asked to do something that he already knows how to do? For example, in a Discrimination Frame Sequence, one of the frames may ask the student to make an identification by writing the name of the object beside each S^D. The value of all of this writing is questionable, since the goal of the frame is to cause the student to make a proper discrimination. Asking him to write the name each time, instead of merely making a check mark, does not necessarily increase the strength of the discrimination he is learning to make. He may simply be getting practice in writing a word with which he was thoroughly familiar before he began the program.

The cues and prompts used in each frame must also be considered. Are they too obvious? Do they cause the student to think, or is the answer handed to him? The ideal sequence starts with a frame containing maximum stimulus and requiring minimum response, and proceeds to a final frame that contains minimum stimulus and calls for maximum response. In each succeeding frame after the first frame, a weaker prompt is used, until the student can perform with no prompt at all. If this procedure is not being followed, something must be done about it.

In this same vein, the programmer must ask himself what a cue and prompt calls attention to in a frame. Is it prompting a relevant item or concept, or is it prompting an item simply to get the student to make a response for the sake of making a response? This, of course, ties in closely with the question concerning relevancy of response. If the item prompted is irrelevant, the student's response will be irrelevant.

Intra-frame step size refers to the amount of material that is presented within each frame of a program. When programmed instruction was in its infancy, it was generally considered by the "in" group that there should be only one idea or one small concept presented in each frame. This line of thought is still considered valid by many people. The response asked of the student should require that he *use* the material in the frame. It should be necessary for him to use *all* of the material presented; and, most often, one response can cover only one idea. If several concepts are presented in one frame and the student is required to consider only one of them in making his response, he cannot be held responsible at a later stage of the program for concepts other than that to which he responded. For an effective program, only one stimulus-response pair of optimum size should be presented in each frame.

Finally, the content of the frame must be considered. Is *all* of the material that is included pertinent? Students have a habit of trying to learn everything that is contained in a frame, at least until they become experienced at taking programs. Throughout their academic lives, they have been required to determine for themselves what is and what is not important in a textbook. As a result, they have a sort of sensing mechanism that lights up "Tilt!" each time they run across an item that looks as if it might be "test worthy."

Because of this sensor, irrelevant material in a frame will be memorized by certain students. It is questionable whether or not this is harmful. It is, to say the least, inefficient. The student should not be asked to make a value judgment as to the importance of material within a program. It is the programmer's responsibility to design the program so that the student is led along a definite path and is required to do those things that will cause him to learn only the items deemed important by the programmer. If enrichment material is to be included in a program, it should be clearly pointed out to the student in some manner or other that he is not going to be held responsible for this information. This can be done by including the material in a panel, by setting it off in a separate paragraph, or in some other manner isolating it from those knowledge items that the student is required to learn. Experienced program-takers learn to rely upon the programmer to teach them what he wants them to know. After several successful encounters with well-written programmed material, they come to the realization that if they do what the program asks them to do and make those responses the program asks them to make, they will have learned the material as quickly, as easily, and as completely as possible.

One of the most revealing programming technique edits that can be performed is to place the program in front of several students and have them jot down their comments on the individual frames as they work their way through the program.

If the programmer gets such comments as "How do you expect me to know this?," "Like I've told you five times already, the answer to this question is . . .," and "What the heck do you mean by this?," he knows that there are inadequacies in his frames. The solution, of course, is to rewrite the frames, making the corrections suggested by the students, until there is no longer this type of reaction.

PRACTICAL APPLICATION

The poorly written frames that follow are provided to illustrate some of the things the programmer must look for in his programming technique edit of frames. For the most part, there is only one problem per frame. In some instances, however, several appear.

Survival depends on the maintenance of a suitable relationship with the nonliving environment. Survival also depends on _____.

---

reproduction

It is highly doubtful that the student will come up with the response "reproduction" in this particular frame. The response that is required of him is irrelevant to the concept presented. More than likely, the programmer has elicited the response "reproduction" several times immediately prior to this frame. But he has introduced a new concept and does not require the student to use this concept in making his response. The student is required only to remember what his last response was. This is an example of a response that is relevant to the program, but irrelevant to the particular frame.

Now multiply the number of spaces between the columns by the number of columns, less 1. We will need two columns in this exercise. Now, subtract 1 from the total number of columns $(2 - 1 = 1)$. Next, multiply this figure (1) by the number of spaces between columns (6). The multiplication would give you $1 \times 6 =$ _____.

6

In this frame, the student is asked to do something he already knew how to do before he started the program. The frame does not ask him to do what he is supposed to be learning to do. It is very likely that the student could multiply 1 × 6 and get the correct answer before he read this frame. However, it is not so likely that he understands the reason for using 1 and 6 in this particular situation. This, the generation of the numbers 1 and 6, is the relevant response, not the solving of the mathematical problem.

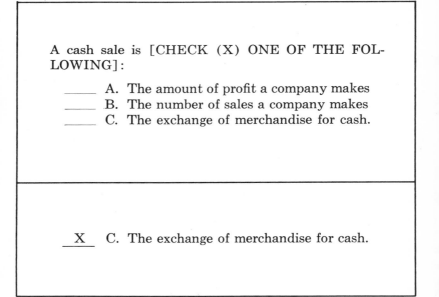

A cash sale is [CHECK (X) ONE OF THE FOLLOWING]:

_____ A. The amount of profit a company makes
_____ B. The number of sales a company makes
_____ C. The exchange of merchandise for cash.

___X___ C. The exchange of merchandise for cash.

This frame is extremely weak in that the S^A's are so obviously incorrect that it requires very little thinking to determine which answer is correct. Frames are supposed to be challenging. If they are not, it is questionable whether they contribute much, or anything, to the program. As another example of an unchallenging frame, consider the frame that follows.

Mrs. Brown went to a large department store and bought a hat for $15.00. She gave the clerk a $10.00 bill and a $5.00 bill. In this example, the $15.00 is the [CHECK (X) THE CORRECT ANSWER]:

_____ A. Merchandise
_____ B. Cash
_____ C. Both of the above
_____ D. Neither of the above

___X___ B. Cash

It is possible to elicit a relevant response with the wrong stimulus, as in this frame.

In a block-style letter, the date, the complimentary close, and the signature begin at the left margin. If letterhead stationery is not used, the return address should also begin at the _____ margin.

left

This frame is an example of a sequential prompt. Applying the yardstick by which the relevancy of a response is measured—*how* does the student arrive at the answer?—it is found that the only possible way the student can come up with the response "left" is by getting a cue from the term "also begins." In this frame, a relevant response is required, but the method by which the response is elicited is weak.

As he writes and reviews frames, the programmer must always keep in mind that he is trying to develop and establish stimulus-response *pairs*. It is not enough merely to have the student make the response "left." The objective is to cause him to make that particular response when presented with a particular stimulus. All of the programmer's efforts should be directed toward the establishment of this relationship.

The frame below is in violation of the rule that the student should be required to use any illustration that appears within a frame.

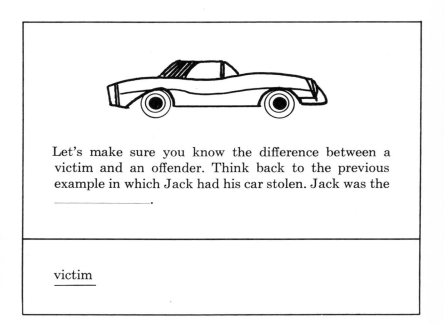

Let's make sure you know the difference between a victim and an offender. Think back to the previous example in which Jack had his car stolen. Jack was the

_____.

victim

The picture of the automobile adds nothing to this frame. The student is not required to consider the illustration in order to answer the frame, nor is the illustration even the slightest prompt to the correct response. Even if the student does look at the picture, he gains nothing and is momentarily distracted from the task at hand.

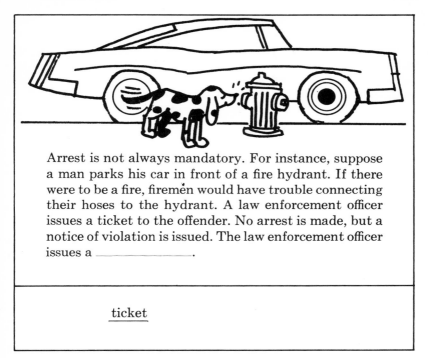

Arrest is not always mandatory. For instance, suppose a man parks his car in front of a fire hydrant. If there were to be a fire, firemen would have trouble connecting their hoses to the hydrant. A law enforcement officer issues a ticket to the offender. No arrest is made, but a notice of violation is issued. The law enforcement officer issues a _____.

ticket

This frame serves to summarize many of the undesirable qualities to be taken out of a frame in the programming technique edit:

1. It is a RAM frame (for "repeat after me"),* requiring only the ability to copy the word "ticket."
2. The illustration is not purposeful, and the weak attempt at humor might be considered in poor taste.
3. The part of the frame beginning with "If there were . . ." and ending with "hydrant" is irrelevant and misleading information. A ticket would be issued even if there were no fire.
4. The response is elicited through a sequential prompt.
5. The apparent purpose of the frame is to establish the fact that a ticket may be a substitute for an arrest. This connection is not made in the frame.

*See pages 126-128 for a more complete discussion of RAM frames.

TECHNICAL ACCURACY EDIT

In an edit of this type, the subject matter expert (two or three SME's, if possible) checks the program to determine whether or not the material presented is technically accurate.

Even a programmer who considers himself an expert in the area he is programming should have his material checked by someone else who is an expert in the field. Too often, a programmer is too close to the bananas to see the bunch. Probably his greatest error will be that of omission. For ease of programming, he may omit certain items. In so doing, he may cause the student to develop an inaccurate concept. This may not be readily visible to the programmer, but it will usually be quite apparent to another SME.

Vocabulary should also be carefully scrutinized. If a definition is being taught, the programmer must be sure it is not one he has modified or simplified to the point of inaccuracy simply for ease of teaching. This is a common tendency—oversimplification resulting in not-quite-technically-accurate material.

HIERARCHY OF EDITING

It should be obvious that all three types of editing cannot be done at the same time. So, the question of which to do first arises. There is a definite and logical reason for performing one type of edit before another: to eliminate wasted effort.

The technical accuracy edit should be performed first. If an item within a program is taught that is technically inaccurate, no amount of composition editing or programming technique editing will correct the situation; what the student learns will still be wrong. By eliminating technical inaccuracy first, time is not wasted making changes that will be negated at a later time.

After a program has been edited for technical accuracy, the next edit is that of the programming technique. Changes required as the result of an edit of this type are generally of major scope. Making changes to programming technique usually negates any editing for composition that has been done, so the composition edit would have to be done over.

Once the programmer is certain that his program is technically accurate and that his programming technique is as it should be, he begins the final edit, the composition edit. An edit of this type will not usually negate any other type of edit, since changes made will be relatively minor in nature. Editing for composition is the final polishing given to a program. It supplies that look of professionalism necessary to instill in the student a proper attitude toward the program.

Basically, editing amounts to knocking the rough edges off and polishing the program. It is the final step before the program is put to the supreme test—placing it in front of a student. It is impossible to eliminate *all* of the bugs from a program through editing. Students will still find things wrong with the program. However, a thorough edit will give it more of a chance for success.

It is much easier on the programmer's ego to discover mistakes in a program through a careful edit than to have them called to his attention by students or by a subject matter expert who is considering the program for use.

It is very difficult to establish general rules by which good frames may be distinguished from poor ones. The purpose of this chapter is simply to point out some of the more obvious, recurring violations of sound programming principles.

13

TESTING

Somehow, no amount of preparation will condition a programmer for the reactions he experiences the first couple of times he tests a program of his own design. But, nerve-wracking as it may be, the testing of the program is one of the most important phases of its development. The program is designed for the students. If it doesn't work with them, it does not do what it was intended to do. No amount of eloquent writing, fancy illustrations, or tricky mechanics can make it a program if it doesn't teach the student— or, more explicitly, if the student doesn't learn by taking the program.

Programmers hold to the axiom that without learning, there is no teaching. Without learning, it isn't a program. The device, or whatever it is, fails to live up to the purpose for which it was designed if the student doesn't walk away from it possessing those terminal behaviors that the program was intended to impart. He *must learn*; and if he doesn't, it is the programmer's responsibility to modify the program as extensively and as often as necessary to reach the desired goal.

TYPES OF TESTING

In this chapter, three types of testing are discussed: one-to-one testing, small group testing, and field testing. Each type is designed for a separate and distinct purpose. It is not a question of testing a program with one or another of the three. All three types of tests are required to uncover all of the inadequacies of a program.

ONE-TO-ONE TESTING

Testing on a one-to-one basis involves the programmer and a representative of the group for which the program is intended (population). With the help of this one student, the programmer attempts to uncover as many program inadequacies as possible and eliminate them from the program.

For testing on the one-to-one basis, it is better to pick a student who is a little slower than the average, since he will probably stumble more often throughout the program than would most of the students. It can be decided later whether the particular blocks over which he stumbles should be removed, or if the majority of the group would not be bothered by them. It is important, however, that these stumbling blocks be pointed out so that there is an opportunity to make this decision.

Before testing on a one-to-one basis is begun, it is important to put the student in the proper frame of mind. It should be impressed upon him that he is going to help rewrite the program. It should be explained to him that the students must learn for a program to be considered successful. He should know that the programmer is looking for, and expects him to point out, areas that are the slightest bit confusing, areas in which he is not sure of his response, areas in which a particular statement is not consistent with a concept he gained from an earlier part of the program, and areas in which the program seems to talk down to him. In short, the student representative must understand that he and the programmer, together, are going to smooth out the program, remove its inadequacies, and make it work—and not necessarily the first time through.

For this type of testing, the programmer develops test copies of his program in a one-frame-per-page format, with the answers either on the back of each page or at the top of the following page. The student is given the first frame and asked to read it and announce out loud what goes in the blank or how he would answer the question. After he has given his answer, the programmer confirms it for him and hands him the next frame to read. While he is reading the second frame, the programmer records his previous answer.

If the student cannot answer or gives a wrong answer, the programmer discusses the frame with him at that time and tries to find out what it is that has led him astray. Many times, the programmer discovers that the smallest items have distracted the student and thrown him off the track. Students don't always think as the programmer imagines they will, and the purpose of this testing is to see how close he came to anticipating and preparing for their mental activities.

In addition, during this testing, the programmer has an opportunity to evaluate the validity of his adjustive devices. He finds out if they have the capability of sensing student inadequacies and make adjustments for these shortcomings.

It is important that the programmer keep copious notes at all times while conducting this type of test. When the student makes a wrong answer, he records this response. Then, after questioning him, he makes a note of the events or concepts that led up to that answer—what caused it.

As the student progresses through the program frame by frame, the programmer will find frames to which the student simply cannot respond, frames that befuddle him completely, and frames that require a great deal of explanation to put him back on the track. These are the stumbling blocks to be eliminated by rewriting the program.

There is no point in giving the student a test after he has taken the program on this one-to-one basis, for the discussion of the program and the help with difficult frames invalidate any results that might be obtained. Testing on a one-to-one basis is merely to ensure that a student can understand what he is reading and perform those tasks required of him as he goes through the program. At this point, the programmer does not know whether or not the program works.

SMALL GROUP TESTING

After the program has been tested several times on a one-to-one basis and revised each time to eliminate inadequacies pointed out by the students, it is time to try the program out on a small group of students to determine how much of the material they learn.

The procedure for group testing is different than that for one-to-one testing in that there is no personal contact between the programmer and the students while the students are taking the program. Five to eight average students are selected as test subjects. Again, it should be impressed upon the students that they are taking a *draft* of a program, one that is still in the developmental stage, and that it is the program that is being tested, not them. The students should understand that they act merely as advisers telling the programmer what is wrong with the program and as a bench mark against which he will measure how well the program performs. However, they should also be encouraged to give the program a fair trial and to try to learn the material.

After his introductory remarks, the programmer administers a pre-test to determine the extent of the students' knowledge in the area before they begin the program. The pre-test will be similar to, if not the same as, the test to be given at the end of the program (the post-test). Since credit can be taken only for the amount of gain that the students make in the program, if the programmer doesn't know their starting points, he cannot tell, on the basis of a post-test, their gains.

The students should be encouraged to guess at the answers on the pre-test, since many times a guess will turn out to be a correct answer—an answer that they knew all the time, but of which they were uncertain. The best test subjects are those who score almost nothing on the pre-test. These students offer the greatest challenge to the program, for they have the most to gain.

After the pre-test, the students are instructed in the mechanics of taking the program. They should be asked to mark the difficult areas or frames in some manner as they work their way through; later, the programmer will discuss these areas with them.

Then, the students are given the programmed booklets and asked to go through the material. The programmer notes the starting time, since he is interested in knowing how long it takes an average student to finish his program. Once the students have started the program, they are not given any help or clarification of the material.

As each student finishes the program, the time at which he finishes is noted and he is given the post-test. His results on the post-test will be an indication of whether or not he actually learned those things that the program set out to teach him.

After grading each student's post-test, the programmer sits down with the student and discusses the program. He leafs through the student's copy of the material and isolates those areas marked as difficult. He discusses each of these areas, trying to determine what program inadequacy caused the student to have trouble.

After all of the students have finished the material, taken the post-test, and been interviewed, the programmer begins his statistical analysis, which is discussed in the next chapter. If the results on the basis of this analysis reach the standards set for the program, he is ready to go on to the next phase of testing. If they do not, he must modify the materials as indicated by the analysis and, using the revised program, repeat the test on another small group.

FIELD TESTING

Once his small group tests have been successful, the programmer is ready to test his program on the population and under the conditions for which it was designed. In this instance, the program will be tested on an entire class within the population or out in the field in an actual job training situation. The teacher or trainer, not the programmer, presents the program to the students just as if it were a normal part of the class routine or training procedure.

Since the programmer does not physically administer the program, field testing gives him an opportunity to test another extremely important aspect of the program, the instructions to the user of the program. The teacher's and the students' roles must both be clearly defined. A valid program improperly administered—or taken—can fail during a field test as readily as a poorly written one. Somehow, either within the program itself or as a separate item, a guide for the use of the program should be supplied for the teacher or trainer. This "administrative guide" should simplify the use of the program, rather than create further problems.

With the field test, as before, all students should be pre-tested and post-tested. The programmer is not interested in whether the students can get through the materials, but in how well the program accomplishes its purpose.

It is important that the students not consider themselves to be part of an experiment, since this might have a tendency to invalidate the test results. As near to normal conditions as possible should be maintained.

The purpose of field testing is to validate a program—to determine whether or not it can do the job. After a large enough group of students has been tested under similar conditions and the test results indicate a successful program, the program can be considered a valid one—one that will work whenever administered to a similar population under these same conditions.

After the program has been successfully field tested and is considered valid, there is no further need to test it. It is then possible to rely on the anticipated results.

During the field test, the programmer expects to find few areas in need of revision, since most of the revision work has been done in the one-to-one and small group testing. Occasionally, however, a program will fail to live up to its standards in a field test. If this happens, there is no alternative but to rewrite the program and proceed once again through the testing cycle. If the rewrite was a very minor one, it is possible that only an additional field test will be required. If, however, the field test indicated that a major revision was in order, and extensive repairs have been made to the material, it may be wise to repeat the entire testing cycle.

GENERAL INFORMATION

At all times during the testing of a program, no matter what phase of the testing cycle, the programmer should keep in mind that the purpose of the testing is to test the program, not the students. If testing goals are not met, the fault lies not in the students, but in the program. It is a great temptation after an unsuccessful test to say, "Well, I just got a bunch of dumb students!" This may be true. It may also be true, however, that students of this type comprise 30 to 50 per cent of the student population for the program. The program should be able to compensate for their inadequacies. If a student puts down that 2 plus 2 equals 5, one of two things has happened: (1) The programmer taught him that 2 plus 2 equals 5, or (2) the programmer failed to teach him that 2 plus 2 equals 4. In either case, it is not the student's fault; it is an inadequacy of the program.

Testing a Branching Program offers a unique situation. This is also true if extensive use has been made of adjustive devices within a program. Whenever the student is given an opportunity to take one of two paths, it is to the programmer's advantage to know which path he takes. In a Branching Program, some of the branches may be found unnecessary—or, more embarrassing, it may be found that *all* of the branches are unnecessary. In either case, the programmer will want to make changes in the program.

Since students do not normally write the answers to Branching Programs, the programmer must, when testing, ask them to indicate in some manner the frames that they have taken. They can do this simply by making check marks beside the answers they select as correct.

Even if a program is designed eventually to be used with covert responses, it should always be tested overtly, since the programmer is interested in the student's answers. An incorrect response will often give the programmer a clue to a program inadequacy. If the student is to work math problems in a program, room should be left in the frame for his calculations and he should be encouraged to make calculations in the space provided. In examining such calculations, the programmer may find that the student set up the problem correctly, but made a simple mathematical error. Normally, unless the program is designed to teach mathematics, the programmer cannot hold the program responsible for this type of error. If a prerequisite to taking the program is a certain level of mathematical ability, no amount of writing and rewriting short of teaching the student mathematics and simple caution will preclude these errors.

14

TEST ANALYSIS

One of the basic premises of programmed instruction is that a program is designed with specific objectives. In order to determine when these objectives have been met, several measurement devices have been used. One of the most common is the 90/90 standard.

THE 90/90 STANDARD

The term "90/90 standard" has different meanings to different programmers. Most programmers have some bench mark to measure performance, however, and they agree that whenever their program reaches this level it is time to stop testing and start printing.

One type of 90/90 standard is met when the students are able to answer 90 per cent of the frames in a program correctly. This does not necessarily indicate—to the authors, at any rate—that the program will do the job for which it was intended. The degree of success of the students—and, consequently, of the program—is what the students are able to do after they have *finished* the program, not what they are able to do while they are going through it. As stated before, the basic principles of programmed instruction require that students make correct responses most of the time. Ninety per cent is probably as good a representation of "most of the time" as any. We do not believe, however, that a program in which any student makes correct responses only 85 per cent of the time is necessarily a bad program if it enables him to do all of those things it set out to teach him. Nor do we believe that a program that ensures 100 per cent success by the student as he works his way through it is a good program if it fails miserably when the student is asked to perform on a post-test.

One way to look at the 90/90 standard is to require that 90 per cent of the students make a 90 per cent gain using the program. The student gains 90 per cent of what it is possible for him to gain, based on his pre-test score. For example, a student pre-tests at 30 per cent. Since the highest possible score he can make is 100 per cent, if the program is 100 per cent efficient, he can gain an additional 70 percentage points. Assuming that he scores 90 per cent on the post-test, he has gained 60 out of a possible 70 percentage points by taking the program. He has a gain of 6/7, or 85.7 per cent of the maximum gain possible for him.

When asked what the 90/90 standard means, many programmers will answer with something like, "It means that 90 per cent of the students get 90 per cent of the material." This sounds reasonable enough, and it is a very creditable goal. But let's stop a moment and analyze this statement. There are several interpretations of this seemingly clear-cut explanation, and there are many ways to bend statistics to indicate that "90 per cent of the students get 90 per cent of the material." One very obvious way is to ignore completely the scores of the lowest 10 per cent of the students. If this is done, we are dealing with only 90 per cent of the students. Then an average is taken of the remaining students' scores. If the average, or mean, of the top 90 per cent of the students is 90 per cent, we have met our criterion. This is one way of looking at it.

Another way of interpreting the 90/90 standard is to say that the group mean must be 90 per cent. The program must be able to do 90 per cent of what it was intended to do. This appears, on the surface, to be a very valid criterion against which to work. However, let's assume that we are using a ten-item test. Each item tests the achievement of *one* of our objectives for the program. Suppose, also, that we are testing the program on a hundred students. If all hundred students miss one specific item—item number eight, for instance—the program has a mean of 90 per cent. However, the program has failed completely on one of its objectives—number eight. None of the students is able to do what this objective says the students will be able to do. It is apparent that a more complete criterion must be established against which to measure programs.

Our interpretation of the 90/90 standard, and the one against which we design programs, is more stringent. The first 90 represents the class mean, considering *all* of the students. The post-tests are graded, the raw scores are given percentage values, and the class mean is found. This class mean must be 90 per cent or better. The second 90 represents the qualification that 90 per cent of the students will achieve each and every objective of the program. If a ten-item test measures every objective of a particular program and we are testing it on a hundred students, no more than ten students (10 per cent) will be allowed to miss any one of the items. If more than 10 per cent incorrectly perform on a particular item, the area of the program that instills that behavior must be revised ("beefed up" or clarified) and the program retested. When we feel certain that on a given population the class mean will be at least 90 per cent and that no more than 10 per cent of the students will miss any one particular item, we then consider that program complete and ready for use.

CRITICAL TEST DATA

There are many types of data that can be gathered concerning a program's performance. Some of it is useful, and some of it is not so useful. Part of the data is gathered directly from the post-test results, and some of it is collected from the students' completed copies of the program itself. The types of data suggested in this chapter are those that will be found helpful, and in some cases essential, to the revision of a program and the determination of whether or not it meets the 90/90 standard.

One of the first items needed is the mean for the post-test. What is the group average? This information is calculated the same as any class average. No statistics should be ignored. All of the students' performances are important, and each indicates some measure of the program's proficiency. The class mean should be 90 per cent if the programmer is striving for the 90/90 standard. If it is, the first criterion is met.

In order to determine his success in meeting the second criterion, the programmer must run a test item analysis. This requires a consideration of each item individually. The programmer must determine whether 90 per cent of his students adequately answered every item. If 90 per cent (or more) have correctly answered each question, the second objective has been met. The statistics indicate that the program works.

There are several other items of information about which the programmer is going to be interested. First of all, he is probably going to want to know what the class range was. What was the lowest score in the class and what was the highest? This information is extracted directly from the test data, and no calculation is involved.

The programmer will also undoubtedly be interested in the amount of time the average student requires to take the program. Along with the average, he will want to know the slowest and the fastest student times. This information is needed if the program is going to be used in a classroom situation, or under circumstances wherein it is necessary to know the amount of time that must be allowed for students to complete the program.

Since each program is usually tested several times, each time adding to the amount of statistics, it is more convenient to keep track of statistics if some type of form is used on which data can be summarized. The form that follows is suggested for use in recording data.

Program Title: _____ **Date:** _____

Number of Students: _____ **Population:** _____

Group Pre-test Mean ____ % **Range** _____ to _____

Group Post-test Mean ____ % **Range** _____ to _____

Time Data: Mean _____ min. **Range** _____ to _____

ITEM ANALYSIS

Item #	Number Correct	% Correct

In numbering test questions for the test item analysis, it is important to consider items that have several parts to their answers. If one of the test items is that the students will be able to list three things, each of these "parts" should be recorded separately. If the students are to be able to list "apples, pears, and oranges," for example, it is helpful to know which particular one they have missed whenever one of the items in the list is missed. If it is not known that the students miss only the "oranges" answer, the programmer may needlessly revise the portions of the program that teach "apples" and "pears." Also, even though it is one objective that the students be able to list the three fruits, each of the fruits is a separate and distinct objective. There is an objective that the students will come up with the response "apples," another objective that they will be able to come up with "pears," and a third objective that they will answer with "oranges" when presented with the stimulus "Name three fruits grown . . . ." The primary objective of breaking each of the test items into the smallest possible parts is to enable the programmer to identify more precisely the inadequate portions of his program—to focus attention on as small an area as possible for revision purposes.

Before beginning to rewrite, revise, or add frames, the programmer should know exactly what he is trying to do. A revision should not be a hit-or-miss affair. The test item analysis should have indicated specific, concrete failures within the program; these areas should be the target for revision.

FRAME ANALYSIS

Frame analysis is a supplementary method by which the programmer can discover additional problem areas within a program. In this type of analysis, he is not so much interested in *percentage* of misses as in *clusters* of misses. As the analysis is performed, he is visually able to identify areas within the program where there appear to be problems.

For the frame analysis, it is convenient to use a form similar to that used in test item analysis. A large sheet of graph paper is probably best for this purpose.

Frame #	Student	1	2	3	4	5	6	7	8	9
1										
2										
3										
4										
5										
6										
7										
8										

The programmer examines the program frame by frame and makes an "X" in the square that represents a miss of that frame by a particular student. He does this for every student's program. This can be a very time-consuming and tedious task, but it is worth it. Problems that are not indicated in test item analysis may be indicated. When the data from each student's program has been extracted, definite patterns of misses will be seen on the form. For example, there may be a large concentration of X's around certain items.

Usually, these clusters indicate a problem area within the program. It seldom happens that there will be problems with only one frame. More often, it will be with several consecutive frames. If it is discovered, for instance, that all of the students missed frame number three, a few missed frame four, all of them missed number five, and a few missed number six, there is an entire area that needs reworking.

In addition to searching for clusters of X's, it might be a good idea to determine the average frame error rate. The frame error rate is the percentage of frames to which a student made an incorrect response. The average frame error rate for the program is the students' frame error rates averaged. Normally, an acceptable frame error rate will run between 5 and 10 per cent. Although the average frame error rate doesn't tell much about how the program performs, for this is determined from post-test results, it does tell how hard the program was for the students. A program with a high average frame error rate will probably not be successful. The students will become frustrated while working the program, and they will finally just stop trying to learn the material. As mentioned before, a program with a 0 or 1 per cent frame error rate is probably not very challenging to students. It is hard to believe a program "challenging" when the students are able to respond correctly to 100 per cent of the frames.

CONCLUSION

There are many ways to extract, compile, and compute statistical information, any one of which may be helpful in determining whether or not a program does what it is intended to do. This chapter does not attempt to supply *all* of the analysis a programmer may want to perform on his program; it outlines the *minimum* effort required if he is to make a comprehensive revision of his program. If a programmer has revised his program and retested it, and if in the second field test he achieved the 90/90 standard we have outlined, he has developed a very good program. This is a difficult standard to meet, but it is worth shooting for. While shooting for it, the programmer should never lose sight of the fact that his *real* standard is 100/100.

A thorough testing and analysis of a program, with appropriate rewrites, will probably constitute one-fourth to one-third of the time and effort that is spent in developing a program.

The testing phase of the program's development is one of the most rewarding, and eye-opening, for the programmer. There is no feeling quite like seeing one's first program "fly." There is something special about running through the test analysis and discovering that you have actually designed a *packaged change of behavior*, one that can be handed to a teacher with the truthful comment that this material can cause his students to learn— that if they go through the material, you guarantee that they will be able to do something when they finish the program that they couldn't do when they started.

AFTERWORD

By now, you are probably becoming anxious to begin using some of the ideas that have been presented in this book. It is appropriate at this time to forewarn you of some of the pitfalls into which neophyte programmers usually stumble. Although we have presented a mechanical approach to programming, we have taken this approach simply to give you a framework on which to build. The development of a smoothly-functioning program is an art.

In order to become an artist, you must have certain prerequisite skills and knowledge. However, these qualities alone will not produce a work of art. A combination of the basic techniques and the individuality and personality of the programmer is required to develop an interesting and functional program. Each program reflects its writer and his way of thinking, just as a novel gives some insight into the character of the author. Often, the beginning programmer ignores this and concentrates too much on the technical development of the program. As a result, one of the basic pitfalls into which a new programmer blunders is the production of a mechanical, uninteresting program.

The first efforts of neophyte programmers invariably follow a set pattern. These programs are similar in appearance, and they all have similar deficiencies.

First of all, the program of the beginner is very definitely written in three-frame sequences. Each sequence will be an entity unto itself, since he treats each individual teaching point as a separate unit, with little thought for what came before or what is to follow. It is often possible to rearrange or remove one of these sequences, or even add one, and the change will not be noticeable to the reader.

Prevalent in a new programmer's material are "repeat after me" frames, commonly known as RAM frames. These are generally reflected in the set frame of the three-frame Constructed Response Sequence. The following is an example of a RAM frame.

Since a corporation is a separate and distinct being, a lawsuit against a corporation is against only the assets owned by the being that is the corporation.

A lawsuit against a corporation is against only the _____ _____ by the corporation.

This particular frame would be followed by a practice frame that would elicit the response "assets owned." After this would come the terminal frame of the sequence. The frame, obviously, requires very little of the student but the ability to "repeat after me." A long series of such frames will result in extreme boredom and a feeling of disinterest on the part of the student. It offers no challenge to the student. Remember that the basic reinforcer behind programmed instruction is success. Without challenge, there can be little success; and, of course, the more challenge in a frame, the more success.

The student should feel that he has actually accomplished something, not merely repeated a phrase like a parrot. The cure for this type of frame is obvious. Make the frame challenging! Make the student work a bit to come up with the right answer; don't just hand it to him.

In an attempt to eliminate the RAM aspects of the sample frame, you might end up with something like this.

Since a corporation is a separate and distinct being, a lawsuit against the corporation is against only the assets owned by the being that is the corporation.

Joe Smith and Henry Brown went into business for themselves. After being in business for a year, their company declared bankruptcy. As a result of the bankruptcy proceedings, Joe Smith lost his house and car by judgment of the court.

Was Joe and Henry's business a corporation? _____
How do you know? _____

Without going back into the "do's" and "don't's" of Constructed Response Frames, it should be apparent that this second frame requires more thinking on the part of the student. It also requires a more thorough understanding of the teaching point you are trying to get across. The student must read and understand the teaching point in order to come up with the right answer.

RAM frames also appear with other programming techniques, such as Discrimination Frame Sequences. A RAM frame in a Discrimination Frame Sequence would use S^D's that are word-for-word repeats of the S^P. Frames of this type require of the student only the ability to recognize a word or phrase when it is repeated. Here again, the weakness of such a frame is its inability to make the student work—to ensure that he thinks.

RAM frames, however, are only one of the problem areas to be found in the work of a beginning programmer. A much more serious problem usually reflected is the lack of continuity mentioned earlier, which is much more difficult to correct.

A program must have a methodical and logical line of development. It must have continuity and cohesion. All of the parts must fit together to make up a homogeneous whole. It must read like a well-written textbook insofar as flow of material and development of ideas are concerned. Give the student meaningful examples that relate the subject matter of the program to the real world. It may also be necessary from time to time to put in enrichment material to bridge the gap between teaching points and to ensure continuity.

Programs have been likened to the old tutorial method of teaching where the teacher sat down with the student and guided him step-by-step to learning. The teacher was ever sensing the inability of the student to understand the material and was constantly making allowances for this inability. Your program, too, should guide the student. It should control him at all times. It should lead him step-by-step through a logical development of the material to mastery. Every step the student takes throughout the program should be toward a specific learning goal—each step building upon previous steps, each one taking him a little farther along the path. The goal for the student should be constantly in sight, and a definite direction should be obvious to him. The material must give him the feeling that the program is taking him along the shortest path to his goal.

APPENDIX

CONSTRUCTION RULES

GENERAL RULES

1. Single blanks should not be continued on the next line.
2. Frames should be contained entirely on one page.
3. Blanks should be placed at or near the end of the frame, if possible.
4. Lists of words should be arranged alphabetically, unless they are commonly used in some other order, such as: more/less, debit/credit, front/back, top/bottom, etc.

DISCRIMINATION FRAMES

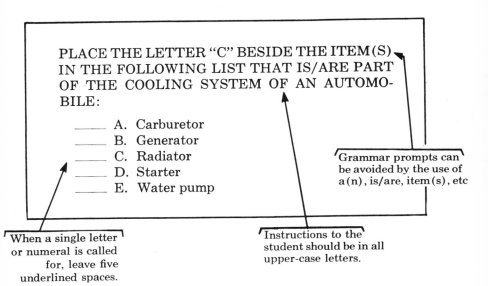

PLACE THE LETTER "C" BESIDE THE ITEM(S) IN THE FOLLOWING LIST THAT IS/ARE PART OF THE COOLING SYSTEM OF AN AUTOMOBILE:

_____ A. Carburetor
_____ B. Generator
_____ C. Radiator
_____ D. Starter
_____ E. Water pump

Grammar prompts can be avoided by the use of a(n), is/are, item(s), etc

When a single letter or numeral is called for, leave five underlined spaces.

Instructions to the student should be in all upper-case letters.

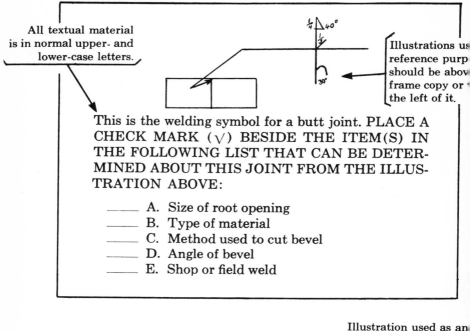

All textual material is in normal upper- and lower-case letters.

Illustrations us reference purp should be abov frame copy or the left of it.

This is the welding symbol for a butt joint. PLACE A CHECK MARK (√) BESIDE THE ITEM(S) IN THE FOLLOWING LIST THAT CAN BE DETER-MINED ABOUT THIS JOINT FROM THE ILLUS-TRATION ABOVE:

_____ A. Size of root opening
_____ B. Type of material
_____ C. Method used to cut bevel
_____ D. Angle of bevel
_____ E. Shop or field weld

Illustration used as an S^D or S$^△$ should be placed below frame co

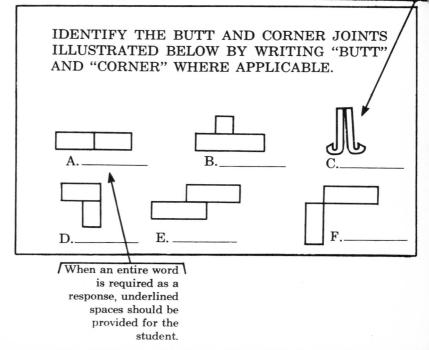

IDENTIFY THE BUTT AND CORNER JOINTS ILLUSTRATED BELOW BY WRITING "BUTT" AND "CORNER" WHERE APPLICABLE.

A._____   B._____   C._____

D._____   E._____   F._____

When an entire word is required as a response, underlined spaces should be provided for the student.

CONSTRUCTED RESPONSE FRAMES

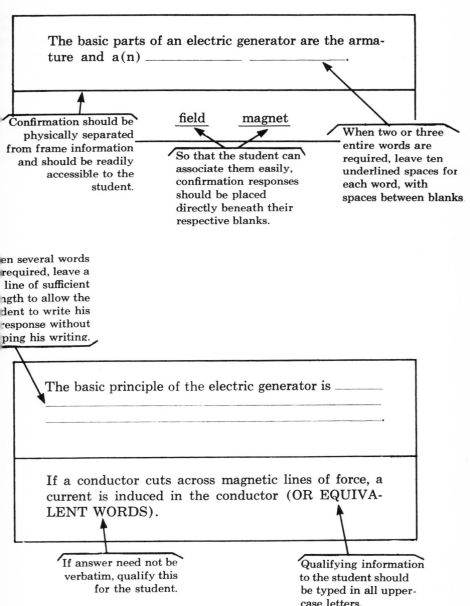

The basic parts of an electric generator are the armature and a(n) _____   _____.

Confirmation should be physically separated from frame information and should be readily accessible to the student.

field   magnet

So that the student can associate them easily, confirmation responses should be placed directly beneath their respective blanks.

When two or three entire words are required, leave ten underlined spaces for each word, with spaces between blanks.

en several words required, leave a line of sufficient ngth to allow the dent to write his response without ping his writing.

The basic principle of the electric generator is _____

_____

_____.

If a conductor cuts across magnetic lines of force, a current is induced in the conductor (OR EQUIVALENT WORDS).

If answer need not be verbatim, qualify this for the student.

Qualifying information to the student should be typed in all upper-case letters.

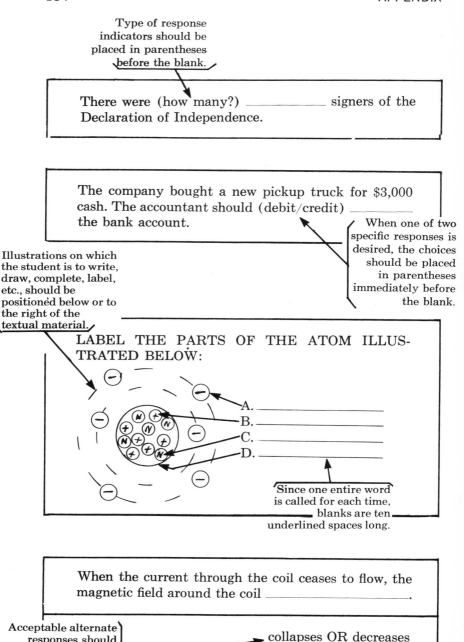

Type of response indicators should be placed in parentheses before the blank.

There were (how many?) _____ signers of the Declaration of Independence.

The company bought a new pickup truck for $3,000 cash. The accountant should (debit/credit) _____ the bank account.

When one of two specific responses is desired, the choices should be placed in parentheses immediately before the blank.

Illustrations on which the student is to write, draw, complete, label, etc., should be positioned below or to the right of the textual material.

LABEL THE PARTS OF THE ATOM ILLUS-TRATED BELOW:

A. _____
B. _____
C. _____
D. _____

Since one entire word is called for each time, blanks are ten underlined spaces long.

When the current through the coil ceases to flow, the magnetic field around the coil _____.

Acceptable alternate responses should appear on the same line separated by the word "or" in upper-case letters.

collapses OR decreases

The colors of the flag are ——————, ——————, and ——————.

red   white

(and) blue   IN ANY ORDER

If the response wouldn't normally be capitalized if used as indicated by the position of the blank, do not capitalize in the confirmation.

If the order of several responses is not critical, inform the student with a qualifying statement in upper-case letters.

You've learned that a Coulomb is a measure of electric charge. For your information only, one Coulomb represents 6.28×10^{18} electrons. NO RESPONSE REQUIRED.

If no response is expected of the student, inform him of this fact in the frame itself, not in the confirmation block.

You should now be able to match the capitals to their respective states. DRAW LINES TO CONNECT THESE CAPITALS WITH THEIR STATES:

hen supplying lists of words, list them alphabetically, if feasible.

California   Albany
Indiana   Columbus
New York   Indianapolis
Ohio   Madison
Wisconsin   Sacramento

Matching may be done in this manner. See next frame for another example of matching.

California   Albany
Indiana   Columbus
New York   Indianapolis
Ohio   Madison
Wisconsin   Sacramento

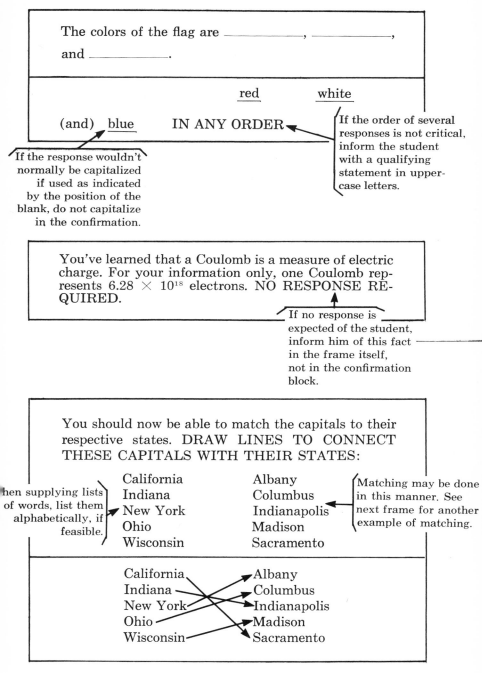

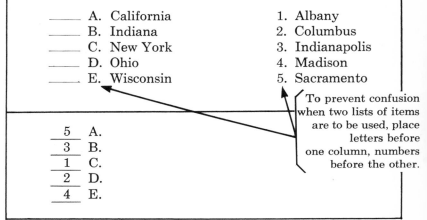

You should now be able to match the capitals to their respective states. PLACE THE NUMBER OF EACH CAPITAL CITY IN THE BLANK TO THE LEFT OF THE APPROPRIATE STATE.

_____ A. California   1. Albany
_____ B. Indiana   2. Columbus
_____ C. New York   3. Indianapolis
_____ D. Ohio   4. Madison
_____ E. Wisconsin   5. Sacramento

To prevent confusion when two lists of items are to be used, place letters before one column, numbers before the other.

5   A.
3   B.
1   C.
2   D.
4   E.

BABOON FRAMES

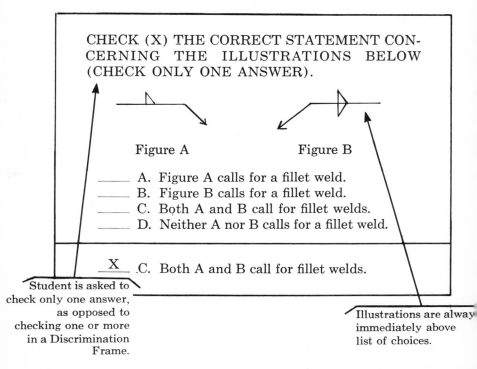

CHECK (X) THE CORRECT STATEMENT CONCERNING THE ILLUSTRATIONS BELOW (CHECK ONLY ONE ANSWER).

Figure A   Figure B

_____ A. Figure A calls for a fillet weld.
_____ B. Figure B calls for a fillet weld.
_____ C. Both A and B call for fillet welds.
_____ D. Neither A nor B calls for a fillet weld.

  X .C. Both A and B call for fillet welds.

Student is asked to check only one answer, as opposed to checking one or more in a Discrimination Frame.

Illustrations are always immediately above list of choices.

INDEX